Essential Skill

Brilliant Family Dog

Book 2

Change for your Growly Dog!

Action steps to build confidence
in your fearful, aggressive, or reactive dog

Beverley Courtney

Books by the author

Essential Skills for a Brilliant Family Dog

Book 1 **Calm Down!** *Step-by-Step to a Calm, Relaxed, and Brilliant Family Dog*
Book 2 **Leave it!** *How to teach Amazing Impulse Control to your Brilliant Family Dog*
Book 3 **Let's Go!** *Enjoy Companionable Walks with your Brilliant Family Dog*
Book 4 **Here Boy!** *Step-by-step to a Stunning Recall from your Brilliant Family Dog*

Essential Skills for your *Growly* but Brilliant Family Dog

Book 1 **Why is my Dog so Growly?** *Teach your fearful, aggressive, or reactive dog confidence through understanding*
Book 2 **Change for your Growly Dog!** *Action steps to build confidence in your fearful, aggressive, or reactive dog*
Book 3 **Calm walks with your Growly Dog** *Strategies and techniques for your fearful, aggressive, or reactive dog*

Your free book is waiting for you!

Impulse Control is particularly valuable for the reactive and anxious dog. Get a head start with your training by developing astonishing self-control in your dog! Change your dog from quick on the trigger, to thoughtful and reflective.

Go now and get your step-by-step book absolutely free at
Brilliant Family Dog
www.brilliantfamilydog.com/freebook-growly

Disclaimer

I have made every effort to make my teachings crystal clear, but we're dealing with live animals here (that's you, and your dog) and I can't see whether you're doing it exactly right. I am unable to guarantee success, as it depends entirely on the person utilising the training programs, strategies, tools, and resources.

What I do know is that this system works!

Nothing in these books should upset or worry your dog in any way, but if your dog has bitten or you fear he may bite, you should take action straight away:

1. Use a muzzle
2. Consult a specialist force-free trainer

"I am not a vet"

You'll see this statement dotted about the book. I am not a vet, but there are some things with a medical slant that I need to draw your attention to.

I do not wish to wake up one morning and find my front lawn covered with angry vets brandishing syringes and latex gloves. On medical matters, take your vet's advice. You may want to seek out a veterinary behaviourist who specialises in this area.

Any opinions I express are based on my best efforts to study the literature, from personal experience, and from case studies. Not gospel, in other words.

Many of the techniques I show you were not invented by me, but I add my own spin. There will be a little repetition of key points from book to book, to ensure that the new reader has some understanding, and serve as a reminder to the rest of us. Ideally all three books should be read in sequence.

All the photos in this book are of "real" dogs – either my own, or those of students and readers (with their permission). So the reproduction quality is sometimes not the best. I have chosen the images carefully to illustrate the concepts – so we'll have to put up with some fuzziness.

Contents

Introduction

You know your dog has a lovely personality. She's smashing at home - loves playing with the children, does what you ask, settles quietly when you're busy. But outside ... or perhaps when visitors come ... you have a different dog. The ruckus she makes when confronted with a strange person, a strange dog, even a strange *bag*, is upsetting for you and frightening for everyone else. She ducks and dives, lunges and surges, barks, snarls, and growls: who wouldn't be alarmed?

We've looked at

- what is happening,
- why it's happening,
- why it's getting worse,
- and what you can start changing to begin the transformation you're looking for.

That's all in Book 1 of this series.

We're now going to go into far greater detail to give you strategies and techniques to avoid trouble (and if necessary to get you out of it!). These strategies will enable you to change *your* mindset, and then change your dog's mindset. If she's to change, then you have to change too!

But nowhere am I going to tell you it's your fault, or your dog's fault, or the fault of your dog's previous owners, or the fault of the alignment of the stars at your dog's birth. Blaming is totally unproductive. You need to start where you are, with what you've got, and move forward from there.

So we will advance in a cheerily positive state of mind! You'll come to see that what I give you are the missing parts of the puzzle, and you'll be able to see why harsher methods recommended to you in the past have not worked.

And why me?

Spending a lot of time, in my training school Good for Dogs, with "the dog owner in the street" - the family pet owner - has shown me how people learn best, what they need to know, and what they actually *don't* need to know. Being blinded by science is not going to make the training more accessible!

Some of these dog-owners were facing problems with their "growly" dog. Some had tried other avenues and not liked what they were told to do to their dog, whom they loved. Others had seen the tv programs and heard the "advice" from fellow dog owners and knew that way wasn't for them, so they sought out a force-free trainer.

Each new person and each new dog offers a new challenge. I've learned to be adaptable and customise my training for the individual in front of me. What I can say is that this system has a phenomenal success rate. Once the owner is prepared to make some changes and put in the necessary flying hours, they invariably get the transformation they wanted. They may need to adjust their end-goals a little, but that's easy to do once they understand their dog better. Perhaps their dog will never be the life and soul of the party - and that's fine. Just don't force him to go to parties!

See how things started working quickly for Fitz:

> "The past few walks I've seen a huge difference in his behavior in general. He notices the other dogs but doesn't make an effort to lunge or struggle, he makes noise but it is not as dramatic. It's a small step in his social issues, but a big relief that he is learning."

So where do I start?

This book, Book 2 **Change for your Growly Dog!** *Action steps to build confidence in your fearful, aggressive, or reactive dog,* stands alone, but you'll get much more out of it if you've first read the first book in this series, **Why is my Dog so Growly?** *Teach your fearful, aggressive, or reactive dog confidence through understanding.* All the gaps in your knowledge - the whys, whats, and wherefores - will be nagging at the back of your mind and will continually interfere with your understanding of the material in this book. So I recommend you go and get Book 1 and read that first. And to make this easier, there's a special offer for Book 1! (Who can resist a special offer?) Complete clarity is my aim.

So these three books are best consumed together, in order.

- The first tells you what's going on and why - and some of this may surprise you. It's essential to understand a problem before attempting to fix it. This section should bring you lots of "Aha!" moments.

- The second book goes into the detail of what you're going to change and how, what approaches will work best, and what you need to make it all work. Lots of Lessons in this section. And much of this will involve change for *you:* exciting!

- And the third gets you out there with your dog, enjoying a new way of walking and interacting with her, and making the scene at the start of this Introduction - mercifully! - a thing of the past. Lots more Lessons here, and Troubleshooting sections to cover all the "what ifs" you'll come up with.

My suggestion is to read through the book first, then while your brain is filtering and processing this information, you can go back to the start and work through the Action Steps and Lessons with your dog.

For ease of reading, your dog is going to be a he or a she as the whim takes me. He and she will learn the exact same way and have similar responses.

There will be just a few occasions when we're discussing only a male or a female, and that will be clear.

So let's get stuck into Chapter 1!

Section 1

Training basics

Chapter 1

Before we embark on the Lessons, there's an important area we need to cover. Read this now and you'll have plenty of time to be sure you and your dog are properly suited and booted before you get started.

Equipment that will help you ... and equipment to avoid like the plague

I'm going to show you not only what equipment you need, but also what equipment you *don't need*, and - importantly! - what equipment to avoid at all costs.

First of all, let's take a quick diversion into anatomy. There is a myth that a dog's neck is somehow different from ours and can withstand the crushing effect of a collar cutting into the throat without any damage whatsoever. This is clearly nonsense. You only have to hear a dog choking as he heaves into his collar or see his eyeballs sticking out, his tongue going blue, and his face creased with the strain to know how wrong this myth is.

In fact, physiologically a dog's neck is *virtually identical to ours*. The trachea, thyroid gland, and oesophagus are all in much the same place. The nerves and blood supply to the brain are similar.

Now, imagine a constricting force on your own neck. What's going to be affected? Your eyes, your throat, your thyroid. lack of blood to the head, distress, fear, pain, and a feeling of being trapped and threatened. Some of these things are temporary, but some can have a permanent effect, and while the damage can be physical, mental damage will also be caused by this pain and aggravation, resulting in stress and anxiety.

Every time this happens, your dog is making a firm association that "walking on a lead means pain and bad things," which can quickly translate to "being outside is dangerous".

So if it's so bad, why on earth do dogs do it?

Dogs, as you'll oft hear me say, are simple creatures. They are doers, and they do what works. They aren't straining to pull you somewhere because they have a secret agenda or want to show you who's boss. They are pulling into their collar because they want to get somewhere and you usually follow them!

When they're very young, they don't have to pull that hard for the indulgent owner to stretch out an arm and follow. How often do you think they have to try this before it's a habit? Once? Twice? How often does a child need to see where the cake is kept to know which kitchen cupboard to head for? Once, I'd say!

When the dog gets a bit older, larger, and stronger, his owner becomes less forgiving, and he has to pull a lot harder. Sooner or later the pulling wears down the owner's resolve, and they follow their dog. Their dog is experiencing considerable pain and anxiety, but owner and dog are now in a vicious circle of pulling and counter-pulling. This is why the lead responsiveness and parking exercises you'll find in the Key Lead Skills are so important to work on. You don't need to pull the lead or yank it. Just don't follow!

It's going to be very hard for your anxious dog to remain calm with a collar digging into her neck - more on why later on.

But my dog is big and strong!

Your dog doesn't need to be large to damage your shoulders with her pulling. A small and determined terrier can exert a lot of force on the lead. If you have a dog who already pulls like a train as soon as the lead is clipped on, then you'll need to dress her in something different while you train her to walk nicely on her collar.

Collars are very useful for attaching ID tags and for quickly holding onto in the heat of the moment, but they aren't essential dog gear. Your dog can wear a harness whenever you're out - provided it's the right kind - or, of course, your dog can wear both.

Collars

Cricket is comfortable in her velvet martingale collar

Some dogs don't like their collar being touched. They've been hauled about on the collar or dragged somewhere they didn't want to go. I'm horrified when I see people literally dragging a fearful and reluctant puppy along behind them on his bum!

Keep this in mind if you have a rescue dog: rescue dogs may have had a boatload of unpleasant experiences and can be very hand-shy. You might see this as they duck and dive when a hand reaches out toward them. They may also try to grab the hand with their mouth or just freeze in position. Remember not to wallow in "Ahh, someone's hit him!" We start from where we are.

You need to begin by changing your dog's view of a collar-hold to a thing of beauty, not fear. Here's an exercise you can do repeatedly, perhaps when you're relaxing after dinner. Keep it brief and fun.

Lesson 2 The Collar Hold revisited (from Book 1)

1. Have a supply of scrummy treats to hand
2. Have one treat ready in one hand, and with the other hand reach out and touch the side of your dog's face - just for a second - then remove your hand, feed the treat
3. Repeat Step 2 until she's happy to let you touch her face
4. Repeat Step 2, but reach and touch the side of her neck - just for a second - then remove your hand, feed the treat
5. Repeat Step 4 till she's happy
6. Repeat Step 4, but touch the collar for a second before feeding the treat
7. Keep going till you can slip a finger into her collar, remove your hand - feed treat
8. Eventually you'll be able to slide your hand softly into her collar, with the back of your hand resting against her neck, and walk a few steps with her beside you before feeding the treat
9. When you reach towards your dog's collar she'll stay still and allow you to hold it then stay with you

Watchpoints:

- This will take as long as it takes. Maybe one session of a couple of minutes, maybe ten sessions - doesn't matter
- Be sure to remove your touching hand before feeding the treat
- Work *very fast* - touch-remove-treat, touch-remove-treat, keep it light and fun
- You are never pulling on this collar, not even gripping it firmly
- The goal is to be able to slip your hand into your dog's collar whenever you need to

In time your dog should see your hand approaching and offer her collar to you, then stay still while you slip your hand in, with the back of your hand resting against her neck. This contact will become very comforting to your reactive dog.

Choose:

The collar should be comfortable to wear, easy to put on and take off, and quick-drying if your dog enjoys swimming. It can be soft webbing, soft leather, or woven fabric - this last is especially useful for fast-growing small puppies as you slot the fabric onto the buckle wherever you want.

For older pups and dogs I prefer snap collars to buckle collars because you can adjust the size millimetre by millimetre instead of being stuck with pre-punched holes. Buckle collars can come undone.

Martingale collars made of soft webbing are particularly useful for sighthounds, bull breeds, and any other dog whose neck is larger than its head. These slip over the head and can fit very loosely on the dog's neck - but once the lead is attached they are impossible to back out of. Adjust this collar carefully, fitting it so it doesn't tighten and constrict the neck. It's not meant to be a choke collar, just not slip off.

11

Any piece of equipment is only as strong as its weakest part - so check clips, fabric, stitching, the soldering on rings, and so on, before you buy. Don't go cheap.

Avoid:

Avoid collars that work by hurting. This includes prong collars, slip collars, chain collars, half-chain collars, choke collars, and *anything* that uses a battery. (An exception to the no-battery rule is the "buzz" collar for deaf dogs, which vibrates like your mobile phone and serves to catch their attention.)

If you have any of these in your armoury, please destroy them - don't pass them on to be used on some other hapless dog. You may have been told that you had to use these barbaric devices in order to gain control over your dog.

Here's news for you: *your dog is going to learn to control herself!* You don't walk with your child handcuffed to your arm - you hold his hand gently and teach him what you want him to learn.

Remember your dog's neck is just as delicate and sensitive as your own neck. Or your child's neck. Thankfully more and more countries are making these instruments of torture illegal.

Harness

Oakley on a loose lead in his comfy harness

Choose:

The harness I personally favour is the *Wiggles Wags and Whiskers Freedom Harness*, listed in the Resources section at the end of this book along with a link to a demo video. You are not so much looking for something to prevent pulling, rather you want a harness designed to promote balance. You are looking for a harness which attaches to a double connection lead in two places - in front and on the back. You want a harness that does not impede shoulder movement, does not chafe or rub, and has the effect of balancing your dog.

The object of using a harness is to prevent the dog pulling into a collar and damaging herself. It can also make Loose Lead Walking a doddle, as the dog has to support herself on her own four feet - without using you as a fifth leg - but it has to be the right sort of harness! Look for one which has the same effect as the one shown in the video.

"But I want my dog to stop barking - I don't want to learn loose lead walking!" Yes, you do. Walking calmly without discomfort and a fight at every step will help you enormously when we come to changing your dog's mindset when she enters the fray of Outside. For a complete step-by-step course, see *Let's Go: Enjoy Companionable Walks with your Brilliant Family Dog,* Book 3 in the series of **Essential Skills for a Brilliant Family Dog** (more info in the Resources section).

Avoid:

Some harnesses are designed to encourage the animal to pull, like a horse in harness pulling a cart or a husky pulling a sled. They aren't unpleasant: they're just not the right tool for this job. Others are sold to prevent pulling. Sadly many of these work by hurting the dog - by cutting under the armpits or by tightening and staying tight. Your dog will soon be pulling through the pain just as she did with her collar.

Head Halters

Coco at 9 weeks happy in his head halter

These require some skill to use humanely, but are useful if your dog continually has her nose on the ground, or has a habit of leaping out at passers-by to grab them. If the dog lurches to the end of the lead and is stopped abruptly, the head collar could cause her head to twist. It's essential that the lead stays loose when she's wearing it, and you don't flick or jerk it. Gentle pressure to turn the head is what you need and this takes a bit of practice. The best way is to slide your hand right down to where the lead clips onto the head collar and move the dog's head from there. This will ensure you don't yank the lead. Sometimes head collars are promoted to keep control of your dog's head so she can't bite anyone.

Many dogs dislike the head halter, largely because it's just been whammed on their face and tweaked. So acclimatise your dog gradually to this new gear, always associating the sight or touch of the head halter with good things - it could take weeks till she's keen to wear it.

As I said above, your dog is going to learn to control herself (exciting!) and I don't recommend these for trying to change a reactive dog.

Choose:

Only use a "fixed" head halter (example, *Gentle Leader*). Some figure-of-eight head collars will slacken as soon as the pulling stops and are safe to use.

Avoid:

A slip halter, or slip collar-halter combination - all of which tighten and stay tight if the dog pulls.

Leads

Leads are much more meaningful than you may think!

Perhaps you see your lead as a controlling device, a way to move or restrain your dog. What we are working on here is to give the control to the dog, so she can exercise *self-control*. We want her to have the choice to keep the lead loose. Revolutionary, I know! So think of the lead as a connection between you and your dog - as well as insurance that she won't end up under a bus. You may be surprised to learn that a loose lead will actually *lessen* the chance of your dog lunging out! Really … more about this later on.

In order to give your dog the freedom to walk easily beside you, the lead must be long enough. Six feet is a good length. If the lead is too short, as soon as she moves an inch she's on a tight lead! Most leads you find in pet shops are ridiculously short - three feet or so.

When you're holding the lead, break that habit of winding it five times around your hand then continually flicking and jerking it! Many people have no idea that they're doing this, but every flick or jab is another nail in the coffin of your relationship with your dog.

The lead should be held loosely in your sensitive hand. If you need to prevent yourself jabbing the lead, tuck your thumb into your belt or pocket to keep your hand still.

If you have to keep your dog on-lead all the time, you'll also do well with a 15-foot long line for when you're in an open space or field. (Don't use this line when you're on the road!) In fact, you'll need this for some of the training we'll be doing. This length is comfortable to handle and gives your dog the freedom to mooch about and snuffle without danger of her running off. It's important to "flake the line" in your hand - to have it in loose bows or figures-of-eight instead of coils that can tighten and trap a finger. It's the same system sailors use for the rope attached to a fishing net - so that it can pay out freely without getting caught, or catch a leg in a loop and take a sailor overboard with it.

More about all this in the Key Lead Skills in a little while.

Choose:

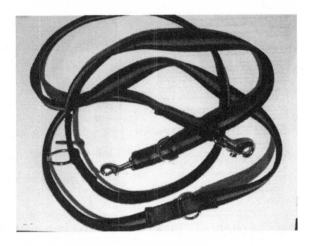

You want a soft fabric or leather lead, at least six feet in length. Some people like a light rope or plaited lead. Remember this is for a dog, not a horse or a bull. The lead needs to be light and comfortable to hold in your hands with no sharp edge to the webbing. A multipoint lead where you can adjust the length of the lead is very useful.

The 15-foot long line is an essential piece of kit for some of the work we'll be doing later on. It will give your dog a choice, and choice is what this training is all about. Have one with a soft woven fabric which won't cut or burn your hands if your dog suddenly zips to the end of it. 1" wide webbing for a larger dog, ¾" for a smaller one, and a handle at the end.

Avoid:

What you do *not* want are extendable leads, bungee leads, anything made with chain, cheap sharp-edged webbing, or a lead less than four feet in length.

Why no extendable lead? These contraptions actually teach the dog to pull! Every time he pulls, he gets more lead. There are also several safety issues around them. I know of cases where the mechanism has broken and the dog has run into the road and been run over. I also know of cases where people have sustained serious burns to their legs or hands - and in one case, their neck - by the cord racing through the mechanism with a heavy speeding dog on the end. And then there are the dogs who panic when the clumpy plastic handle is dropped and bounces along the road behind them as they flee into danger.

The worst thing is that there is no sensitivity or sense of connection through a plastic handle. It may look like a clever idea, but in fact it's a lazy and ineffective option, and totally unsuited for working with a reactive dog.

You have only one chance to make a good first impression

A word about appearances: colours are more important than you may imagine! If the barking dog surging towards you is wearing a red or black harness, you are more likely - according to research into human psychology - to be afraid than if the same dog were wearing a soft pink or turquoise harness. You are more likely to be favourably disposed towards a dog in a pretty flowery collar than one wearing a heavy leather buckled affair with studs. If the owner loves his dog enough to choose pretty colours for him, then there's a chance this dog isn't all bad. Others are therefore less likely to stare at the dog as he walks along the pavement - and staring, as many of you know already, will put a reactive dog on edge. If your dog is a bit butch-looking, or is one of the currently taboo dogs, consider a pretty bandana or a light patterned jacket to present him to the world. Choose dog gear carefully!

People always mistook Lacy as a puppy for a fearsome brown bear cub. And she can look very menacing when in full flow. So she wears a shocking pink collar and harness, and her many leads are all varieties of pink. They'll see her as a pretty girl if it kills me!

Devices used by the Inquisition

By now I hardly need tell you to ditch anything that uses fear or intimidation to get results. So into the bin goes anything you throw at your dog, rattle at her, squirt at her, or anything which uses a battery. *

Please destroy these things - don't pass them to another dog owner!

This is your friend you want to enjoy walks with, not an enemy who has to be kept under control with threats and abuse!

When I've explained how leads and collars work to the owners of a dog I'm working with, I'm always pleased when they tell me they've put all the inappropriate items in the bin - so that no-one in the family can use them again on their family pet.

* This specifically excludes "buzz" vibrating collars for deaf dogs.

Muzzle

Now there's a heated subject! People tend to think that a dog wearing a muzzle must be all bad, and is dangerous. In fact the dog wearing the muzzle is the safest dog, as his armoury is behind closed doors! Sometimes dogs need to wear muzzles because they have a habit of swallowing stones, slugs, or food which makes them ill. The only danger they offer is to themselves. So presuming that a muzzle means a dog is bad is a big mistake.

I can understand you not wanting your barking, lunging, dog to wear a muzzle in case people think she's a dangerous dog. Guess what? They already do! But if there is any history of biting, or just snapping at people, *you* will feel much more relaxed if she's muzzled. As you will learn soon, you being relaxed is a very important part of the training we will be doing. And, of course, if your dog has a bite history - of people, dogs, cats, whatever - it is your duty to protect others and muzzling her is certainly going to do that. Any greyhound that has ever been raced or coursed should always be muzzled when out (as is the law in some countries) to preserve the safety of small fluffy things - be they cats, rabbits, or small dogs.

The first thing to know is that a muzzle can be your friend. If your dog is afraid of people, it's a great way to keep them away! Few people are going to approach your muzzled dog and try to pat her or lean over and stare at her - all big no-no's for the people-reactive dog.

Don't just buy a muzzle and stick it on your dog expecting her to be happy with it. As with the head halter, you need to slowly acclimatise her to love wearing it. You can start with some sort of basket or a paper coffee cup you can cut holes in. Make it a game for her to put her nose into it for a treat! In the Resources section you will find a link to a complete sequence to teach your dog to enjoy wearing a muzzle.

And don't fear that your dog will look nasty. You can get muzzles in pretty colours, and you can attach bows or stickers to them to make them look fun. Lacy's muzzle is black, but has shocking pink bows and ribbons on, to go with her hot pink harness, lead, and collar. Nobody need doubt that she is a girl, and a much-loved pet!

Lacy's pretty muzzle

Choose:

A basket muzzle, which enables your dog to drink, pant, bark, and take treats. If you can find the right toy, they can also pick those up through the bars. A soft rubber muzzle is preferable to a wire muzzle - which can still deliver a mighty bruise when it whacks your leg. The muzzle should fit comfortably round the face, with no pressure under the eyes. It is possible to use a head halter with a muzzle.

Avoid:

A cloth muzzle, or anything that keeps the mouth shut. These are designed for quick application in the vet's surgery, and only for very short lengths of

21

time. The dog is unable to pant. Beware a constricting muzzle on a brachycephalic dog (squashed-nose dog, like a bulldog or pug) - even at the vets. They can't breathe properly - this can end badly.

In this chapter we have learnt that

- Some equipment will help you
- Some equipment will hinder you
- Some equipment should be universally illegal
- We need to face up to the reality of the situation and ensure everyone is safe

Chapter 2
Rewards - what, how, when?

Rewarding your dog with something he really likes is essential to this easy method of training. This may be with a game of chase, tugging with a toy, racing after a ball, being given his dinner bowl, a cuddle, or a tasty treat. It's up to you to find out just what your dog likes (as opposed to what you think he likes) and reward him appropriately when he makes a good choice.

Treats are not a moral issue. They are a means to an end. The end is your dog responding to you and working with you. If employing a few bits of cheese means that my walks are enjoyable and my dog is calm and happy, then that seems a good deal to me. I only give my dogs a treat when they've done something I like: I aim to get through a lot of treats every day!

The treats need to be very tasty - your dog has got to really want them! And you don't want her chewing and chomping on a biscuit for so long that she forgets what she earned it for. So the treat needs to slip down quickly and make your dog think, "Wow! How can I get some more of that?" Your dog needs to know what you like and what does not work with you.

So every time she does something you like, you can mark it by saying, "YES!" and giving her a treat. There is no need for your dog to sit in order to receive a treat. Some dogs think that sitting and begging is the only way to earn a treat, so they sit and beg and annoy at every opportunity. If you are crystal clear about what your dog is doing that is earning the reward (by saying YES), then he will know what actions to repeat, and what doesn't pay. The sitting, begging dog has no idea what causes these random treats to appear.

When you mark an action, you want to mark *as the dog is doing it.* If you are marking a Sit, for instance, you need to say Yes as the bum is going to the floor. If you wait till your dog has already sat, she's now gazing out of the window and thinking of something else. That's not what you want to mark! As the sheepdog trainer John Holmes told us, you need to catch your dog *with his mind down the rabbit-hole,* not wait till he is down the rabbit-hole, when it's too late. You want to catch your dog *thinking* about sitting.

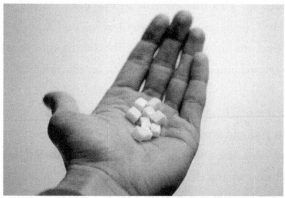

Small, tasty, treats!

Good treats

- Cheese
- Sausage
- Ham
- Chicken
- Frankfurter
- Salami
- Homemade sardine, tuna, or ham cookies
- Freeze-dried 100% meat treats
- Dehydrated liver, heart, lung, etc

...real food in other words. Ideally, they slip down quickly so your dog wants more. Cut them up small - just pea-size will do nicely.

OK treats

- High-quality grain-free commercial treats

Fairly rubbish treats

- Your dog's usual kibble (She gets it anyway. Why should she have to work for it?)
- Cat biscuits
- Dog biscuits
- Stuff of unrecognisable composition sold as pet treats
- Anything you wouldn't put in your own mouth

Do you work more enthusiastically for £60 an hour or for 50p an hour? Quite so. Your dog is the same. Be sure the treats you're offering are worth working for!

How many treats?

It's at this stage that someone usually pipes up and says, "But I don't want to have to bribe my dog. I want him to do it because I say so." Good luck with that, is what I'll respond. Do you get paid to go to work, or do you do it because your boss tells you to? How would you feel if on Friday afternoon your manager said, "You've worked well this week, but I'm not going to bribe you any more so there'll be no pay-check." Would he be seeing you on Monday?

And we're not bribing here. We're rewarding. There really is a big difference. If you wave a treat in front of your dog's nose in order to get his attention, yes - that is a bribe (aka luring). And what do you do if he says "No thanks,

I'd rather carry on chewing your chair leg"? If you can get your dog interacting with you and trying new things to see what will pay, you can reward what you like and ignore what you don't like. And that - you will remember - is the mantra I gave you in Book 1!

Reward what you like
Ignore what you don't like
Manage what you can't ignore

How often do you feed your dog these tasty morsels? That depends on how often you interact with him and how many good responses you can get. There is no time when my dogs may not earn a treat from me, and no place where rewards are not available. So I'm "training" all the time. I prefer to call it conversing or interacting - just like you do with your children. This is real life, not school.

If you're concerned that your dog may gain weight with all these rewards, there are two things you can do. One is to remove an equivalent amount from his dinner bowl, and the other is to use non-food rewards. You want to aim to use non-food rewards *as well as* food ones. Food is very important to all animals, and is the quickest way to teach a lot of new things. You'll also need to teach your dog to enjoy other rewards too: toy play is a big one to encourage.

Of course, if you have a Border Collie he may far prefer toy play as his reward. In that case you'll have to teach him to love treats too, as there are times when play is an inconvenient or inappropriate reward.

You can actually teach this pleasure in both treats and play by giving the less-desired reward, marking with Yes, and immediately following with the favoured reward. You're rewarding your dog for accepting your "inferior" reward. And as you will see as you work with choice training, the cue and the action will become as valuable as the reward that follows. There's fun in store for you!

Start making a list of all the things your dog *loves*. Then highlight all the things he loves that are suitable to be used as a reward. While you're at it, make a note of which he considers the most heavenly reward possible (chasing a toy? a whole sausage?) and which are rather more ordinary rewards - perhaps useful for when you want a slower, more thoughtful, response.

Now when you're in a highly-charged or very distracting situation, you can pull out the heavy artillery. When you're at home and it's quiet, perhaps a lower-value reward will work well. For some dogs, training with dried sprats as rewards is so stimulating that they can completely lose the plot. For others it has to be something as good as a dried sprat to get them to sit up and take notice.

Let your dog tell you what he likes best! If he loves car-rides, then do a moment's training with him just before you grab your keys and take him out to the car. If he loves dozing in a patch of sunshine, you can play some games then open the door to the garden or the south-facing room with the square of sunlight on the floor.

We are different. Our dogs are different. We all learn at different rates. It's up to us to get to know our individual dog and know what makes him tick.

What sort of play?

Play can be anything you and your dog find fun - without any undesirable side-effects such as ripped sleeves and scratched legs. (A licked face is part of the fun.) So for the purposes of this book, I am confining play to fun interaction between owner and dog (as opposed to dog and dog, or dog and toy) which lifts our spirits, causes tails to wag, and builds the bond between us.

The best play simulates one of your dog's instinctive drives. Then you get total immersion in the game - total commitment. All dogs have the same basic instinctive drive: to locate prey, stalk it, chase it, catch it, and kill it. So we'll hijack this sequence to make the best game of all: Tug!

Whatever you've heard about tug being dangerous, giving power to the dog, teaching them to bite, and so on, is all a fallacy. Research (and I mean proper scientific research at a University) has shown that playing tug does not make dogs aggressive. I find the opposite to be the case. If you teach games with lots of impulse control built in, your dog is learning to control herself all the time you are playing. So when you play you teach your dog to grab the toy where you hold it on the floor - not in the air hanging from your hand - to pull as if her life depended on it, to let go when you ask (try holding a piece of cheese to her nostrils for a quick release) and to wait for you to whack the tug on the floor again before grabbing it.

This is a reflection of what they'd learn from their mother when she taught them to hunt. If the pup flies in gung-ho at the first sight of the prey he's likely to stay hungry. A little self-discipline and control will make a hunt fruitful.

A great game for high-speed chasing and catching is a flirt pole. A long, flexible, pole - a carriage whip is perfect - with a soft toy tied to the end of the cord (my current toy is the limb of a teddy bear - "current" because the toy does get shredded) will give hours of fun. Your dog will race like the wind, her sides will be heaving, her eyes will sparkle! And all the while you are teaching her impulse control - how about that!

What's a clicker and do I have to use one?

A clicker is a little gadget you hold in your hand and click to mark the very second your dog is doing something you like. The click is always followed by a treat. It's an excellent way of teaching - especially teaching complex and accurate actions.

But no, you don't need to use one. If you want to work on more complex things like tricks or dance moves, do a bit of reading up on clicker training first to make sure that you do it right. For now, your hands are going to be full enough with lead, treats, and perhaps gloves if it's cold, so don't worry about it.

You should still mark something you like, though! Marking gives the dog the precise information of what it was that earned her a reward and what she needs to do in order to get rewarded again.

Just as effective at indicating your pleasure at what your dog is doing is to say "YES!" enthusiastically. The advantage of a verbal marker is that you'll never leave your voice at home. Say it quickly, at the very instant she does the thing you like. She'll start trying things out to see what makes you say Yes. Now the training is truly interactive.

In this chapter we have learnt that;

- What you reward is what you'll get
- The strength of the reward affects the enthusiasm your dog will deliver
- There are lots of ways to reward your dog for things you like
- A marker word or sound is needed to pinpoint precisely what it is you're rewarding

Chapter 3
Confidence building

Impulse Control

We mentioned impulse control in the last chapter. And there's nothing more empowering than being able to control yourself - and consequently other people and even the situation you find yourself in. Impulse control encourages thoughtfulness, reflection, independence, and builds the ability to make good decisions.

It's what distinguishes the self-centred child from the mature adult. And yes - our dogs can also be mature and make good decisions in the face of great temptation. Think how easy everything else will become when you have a dog who is totally clear about boundaries, is polite and respectful. Think how nice it is when your teenager reaches that stage!

For a deep study of Impulse Control, take a look at the second book in the series **Essential Skills for a Brilliant Family Dog:** *Leave it! How to teach Amazing Impulse Control to your Brilliant Family Dog* which takes you step-by-step through a program to enable you to leave food anywhere in the house in the sure knowledge that it will still be there when you return. It then shows you many other ways your dog can use his new skills to make life easier for you. As you'll expect by now, the methods are all force-free. You'll find more info in the Resources Section.

Responsiveness

In order to have a conversation with someone, they have to be listening. So bleating at your dog who is focussed on something in the distance (on the planet or in his mind) is not going to get you very far. We need our dog to be ready to listen whenever we ask.

So make sure you have got the two games and the Key Lead Skill in Book 1 going well:

Lesson 1: The Precious Name Game
Lesson 2: The Collar Hold
Key Lead Skill no.1: Keeping the lead loose

Don't worry! these also appear in this book in case you missed Book 1. There are a lot more coming in the next chapter, but you need these fluent and fun first.

Tricks!

If your time with your dog is turning into a time of apprehension and worry, there's nothing better to get you both working together - happy and carefree - than to teach a few tricks! There are some great trick training books (see Resources Section) that can get you started. These will build your and your dog's confidence massively. He will enjoy doing something that makes you smile and guarantees a reward. And you can enjoy working with him on something that holds no conflict.

If your dog is people-friendly, he'll like making your friends and visitors smile too! A well-learned trick, like a Sit Pretty, or a Spin, will give your dog something else to do to take his mind off things if he's mildly worried about his environment. Once he's focussed on you and his trick he'll be able to block out the things that are making him anxious.

Isn't this the perfect way to show off your lovely dog! As one student said to me:

> "It's so nice to be able to show that my dog isn't all bad - she just has difficulties in some areas."

ACTION STEP 15:

Choose a very simple trick, teach it at home, then see if you can get it working perfectly everywhere over the next couple of weeks.

Nosework

Dogs' noses, as you probably know, are millions of times more sensitive than our sorry human noses. Let's put those noses to work! Sniffing is a very satisfying canine activity. It lowers the heart-rate and, as you'll remember from Book 1, it is a calming signal to any other dogs around.

So start with simple search games: partially hide a favourite toy - poked under the corner of a carpet, for instance, with part of it sticking out. This minimises the amount of sight being used to find the toy. You'll gradually hide the whole toy in the same place, then moving to different places in the room. Don't be tempted to go from kindergarten to university level in one session! Keep making it easy and fun, and your dog will gradually let his nose take over in the search. You'll hear the vigorous sniffing when that happens!

When you move to the garden, there are a lot more exciting smells out there. There's also weather. Even a slight drift of air can move the scent around a lot, especially in an enclosed area where it will tend to swirl. So go back to the beginning and make it very easy for your dog to succeed. Partially hide the toy under an old flowerpot, for example. Don't hide it in your delicate flowerbed!

Once your dog is good at defaulting to scenting to find things instead of just relying on his eyes, there'll be no more lost balls on walks! And finding hidden children in the house just by scent is always a very popular game: can you imagine the excitement?

You can move on from searching to tracking, where you can lay a strongly-scented track by shuffling along from a start marker for maybe ten yards (fifteen yards if you have a large dog) - lining up with a tree or building in the distance. Show the dog you're placing something between your feet (a favourite toy or large tasty treat), then step out from the track, head back in a big curve, and set off with your dog on a lead or line (preferably connected to a harness). Always be sure you know exactly where the track is - dewy grass or snow is great for this. Only gradually incorporate gentle turns and ordinary strides instead of shuffling.

ACTION STEP 16:

Find out just how clever your dog is by starting some search games with him. Make them hugely exciting and fun. You can play mini search games (toss a toy, or just a stick or fir cone that you've handled, into the long grass) when you're out and about which will help him to keep his mind off the things that worry him, by giving him a job to do.

Distance

And here comes the big one!

Whenever your dog is unhappy about a situation, the first thing to do is make distance.

(This should be in flashing lights and accompanied by sirens and awoogas.)

You need to be working at a distance at which your dog can cope. So if you see a dog or a black plastic sack up ahead - whatever worries your dog - and she is getting twitchy about it, turn and back up a bit. Maybe 10 yards, maybe 50 yards. "Can you look at it from here?" you can ask her. Get to a place where she can view the hazard without stress, and is able to switch her focus easily to you when asked. Then you can consider moving closer. Maybe 1 yard closer, maybe 5 yards - "Can you look at it from here?"

You will be able to establish a distance at which your dog can view the "trigger" (the thing that sets her off) so you know where to start from. This distance can vary, of course, depending on the severity of the threat, whether it's advancing towards you, whether it's making a noise, whether it's moving fast, whether it's windy, what you had for breakfast - and so on. But it gives you a starting point. Gradually the "safe" distance will become automatic for you. You'll be able to gauge how far you need to be from this particular trigger on this particular day.

You'll be able to turn with a cheery "Let's go!" and head away. In calm and quiet. What bliss!

If you were terrified of spiders, would it help to have to walk through a whole lot of them - on the ground, dangling from bushes, flying on the breeze in front of you? Would you trust the person who is trying to force you to "face your fear"? Would you not feel much happier if you could make a choice to turn away as soon as you see all those spiders? This is what you'll be doing for your dog. Your aim will be a calm dog - nothing more.

Personal space

We all have a "personal space" into which only very familiar people may venture. If a stranger approaches you and stands right in front of your face you are going to feel very uncomfortable. You'll most likely take a step back. You may avoid giving them direct eye contact in case it encourages them. You could feel agitated and keen to move on.

On the other hand, if a stranger approaches you with a brief soft-eyed glance and smile, averts their gaze, slows down as they approach, stops a couple of yards from you and shifts their bodyweight back, you will feel much less threatened.

Your dog is the exact same! Only his personal space is way bigger. If I were walking my (reactive) dog and saw you and your dog coming towards us, and I wanted to ask the way to the station, I'd stop way further back than I would if we were both dogless. That may be five yards, or ten yards if it's not too crowded and noisy and I can call out my request to you.

If I were to come to a comfortable position for two strangers without dogs to meet - maybe three yards - this would be much, much too close for my dog, and perhaps yours too. While attending to your answer, I would be failing to notice my dog - who could be going through her entire repertoire of calming signals. As the other dog doesn't move away (because he can't) and I don't move her away (because I'm not paying attention) there may be a sudden flurry and noise from down there at pavement level.

Get used to the fact that your dog's safe distance from a stranger or threat is miles bigger than our safe distance. Make allowances, and keep her calm!

Something new appears near us

This has a fancy name - Sudden Environmental Change. It just means that something new has appeared and it may alarm your dog. It will especially alarm any of the guard, guardian, or herding breeds, who have been bred to notice anything that shouldn't be there. We looked at this early on in Book 1.

If you have a reactive dog you'll become accustomed to "sweeping" the environment to check for UXBs (that's "unexploded bombs" for those of you who watch different tv programs from me!). You'll be looking for whatever your dog is known to react to - dogs, only black dogs, only running dogs, people in hats, all people … etc, and you'll also get into the habit of checking for sudden new things. This could be somebody walking behind you and catching up with you. It could be a pile of garbage left out for the binmen. Or a dog suddenly appearing up ahead.

I'll be giving you techniques to defuse these UXBs quickly and quietly. But you have to notice them first! We're taller than our dogs, so we tend to see things first. If you can notice and act accordingly, you can forestall a reaction. Your dog's confidence will grow when he's not endlessly getting frights.

One thing after another

This is something that can unnerve any of us. Picture this: you're in the kitchen preparing dinner - in a bit of a rush as one of the family needs to go out. You've got everything nicely under control when the phone rings. As you dry your hands and head for the phone, there's an urgent knock and shout at the door. Caught between the two, you hear your pan boiling over! Whoever you speak to next is likely to be snapped at!

This is known in the trade as "Trigger Stacking". You could cope with the rushed meal preparation. At any other time you could cope with a phone call, or a knock at the door. But all at once is too much!

This may account for the big puzzle of why your dog barks at something one day and passes it by at other times. Maybe he sees a dog in the distance, then he hears someone shout over to his left - just behind him a screaming child is approaching on a bike: boom! - it's all too much. He doesn't know what to do so he does his best to keep them all away from him in the only way he knows: barking, shrieking, lunging, bouncing ...

ACTION STEP 17:

So here is a new mantra for you (not quite so new if you read Book 1- but its huge importance makes it totally worth repeating and emphasising here):

Show your dog that he never has to meet another person or dog in his life.

Yes - one day he may want to. But for now, we are not going to put him through this trauma. So when you see ahead of you something that is likely to upset your dog, you wait till he's clocked it, give a cheery "Let's go!" and head off in another direction. What relief your dog will experience! What trust will she put in you now! What a confidence-builder this is!

Responsibility

While you are working on helping your dog overcome her fears you have a huge responsibility to keep everyone else safe.

ACTION STEP 18:

If your dog has a bite history, or you fear losing control of your dog and think he may bite, there is no off-lead exercise for him outside your property or a private fenced area, and he must wear a muzzle when out. More on how to achieve this in upcoming chapters.

In this chapter we have learnt that

- Building your dog's confidence in herself - as well as in you - is key
- There are lots of ways we can do this
- Distance is of critical importance
- Distance comes in many shapes and sizes
- It's up to us to ensure our dog cannot inflict damage

Chapter 4
Let's get cracking!

Lead Skills

You may think that the lead is there to control your dog. You may have been told that you need to control your dog, to make him do things, and to forcibly prevent him from doing other things. But as you'll remember from Book 1, we are not working that way!

What we are doing is giving the dog a choice. Being able to exercise a choice allows your dog a measure of independence which he needs in order to be able to make good choices in the future.

When dressing a small child, a lot of conflict can be avoided by saying, "Would you like to wear your red jumper or your blue jumper?" Note that there's no mention of fairy princess dresses, superman outfits, or ... nothing at all. You have already narrowed her options down to what you would like her to wear today. So you don't care which way she chooses. When your toddler decides which jumper she's going to wear she'll stick to that decision because she made it! Being presented with a straight choice simplifies the task for her and teaches her how to analyse problems and come to a conclusion.

Similarly, when your dog is on the lead and he pulls ahead: instead of yanking the lead and hauling the dog back beside you, you stand still and offer the dog a choice. "Would you like to come back here, or would you rather stand still all day?" You know you can outwait your dog, so you don't mind which way he chooses. After a bit of resistance your dog will work out how to get you moving again and slide back into position. I'm assuming you've already taught him where he should be when you're walking! If not, take a look at the third book in the **Essential Skills for a Brilliant Family Dog** series: *Let's Go! Enjoy Companionable Walks with your Brilliant Family Dog,* which you'll find in the Resources section.

Changing *your* view of the lead is the first thing to do. Your dog may be a determined puller on the lead. This pulling has nothing to do with trying to rule you! Dogs like to get places faster than our miserable slowcoach speed, and if fear is added to this, they'll want to go even faster.

Our necks vs their necks

As we saw in Chapter 1 (the very first thing you learnt in this book!) physiologically, our necks are virtually identical to dogs' necks. So a force tightening on your dog's neck or pressing against his throat is going to have a similar effect on him as it would on us.

Not only do you want to avoid the pain this involves on a dog who is pulling on his lead, but it's essential to remove the anxiety associated with this pressure in order to help your reactive dog view the world with equanimity. So the first step is to use a non-aversive harness (see Chapter 1 and the Resources section) and a comfortable lead of at least 6 feet in length, and the second step is to learn how to use the lead effectively and kindly to get the best possible results.

So your lead is not for yanking or pulling your dog around. The lead is a connection between you, and at the same time a way to stop your dog running into trouble. I'm going to show you a total of six **Key Lead Skills**. Once you know these and you've assimilated them into your daily interaction with your dog you'll wonder how you ever managed without them! I suggest you bookmark this page (that's easy to do on an e-book!) and learn one at a time, coming back for the next one when you've mastered the first.

It may surprise - nay, astonish! - you to learn that if you keep the lead loose, your dog will keep it loose too. Really! It takes two to tango, as the saying goes, and it takes two to have a tight lead. One of us has to stop pulling, and as we're the ones with the bigger brains, it needs to be us.

Your anxious dog's reactivity is going to be massively increased by pulling into her lead. Let's start the change.

You never have to pull your dog's lead again!

Here's an exercise for you to change this entirely. You will recognise it from Book 1. You needed to learn this one as soon as possible, but I'm also including it here so you have all the Key Lead Skills in the same place for easy reference. You can learn this skill in the kitchen first, then graduate to the garden before trying it on the road.

Key Lead Skill No.1
Holding the Lead

1. Have your dog on a longish lead (at least 2 metres)
2. Stand still and let the dog pull to the end of the lead, wherever she wants to go
3. Keep your hand close to your hip. Tuck your thumb into your belt if necessary
4. Wait. Wait till the lead slackens the tiniest bit. It doesn't matter why. You may think you'll need to wait forever, but it's usually only 20 seconds or so at most
5. As soon as you feel the lead relax - for any reason at all, don't judge - call your dog happily and reward her with a tasty treat at your knee
6. Repeat till she understands that it's up to her to keep the lead loose

This exercise is simplicity itself. It tells your dog that you are no longer the one that's pulling. Your hands are soft. It's her choice if she pulls. Given a little time, she'll choose not to pull at all.

If your dog is in the habit of lurching to the end of the lead as soon as it's on, you may have to repeat this exercise frequently. In most cases we need repeat it only long enough to get the new system of lead-holding into our own heads. Once we've got it, our dog will get it.

Remember, dogs are doers, not not-doers. So your dog is learning to keep the lead loose, rather than not to pull on it. See the difference?

What you accept is what you get

Every time you put the lead on your dog, you need to remember to keep your hand close to you and wait for *her* to slacken the lead. If you are in the habit of putting on the lead and letting your dog pull you to the door, then that is what will happen.

What you reward is what you get

There are few better rewards for most dogs then heading out through that door! Your dog needs to learn that - no matter what happened in the past - things have now changed, which means pulling on the lead will get her nowhere. Dogs aren't dumb. They do what works.

From now on you will never move until the lead is slack. NEVER! If you find your arm floating out, recapture it and tuck it into your belt! If it keeps happening, put one of your children on "arm-watch." They'll love having the chance of pointing out your mistake to you!

Time to keep still

Once your dog has learnt to keep that lead loose, and stay more or less near you, you can start on the next Key Lead Skill. It's incredibly useful and keeps your dog calmly under control without any effort from either of you. If you want to stop and chat to someone, make a purchase in a shop, or wait at a bus stop, you can put the handbrake on and park your dog. This is a great way to immobilise your dog without any vestige of force or anger. And it removes from your reactive dog the need to be on duty, watching, guarding, worrying. This is how you do it:

Key Lead Skill No.2
Parking

1. The first thing is to hold your dog's collar. Rather than waving your arm about trying to catch the collar on a leaping dog, simply run your hand down the lead till you reach the collar, and slip a finger under it.
2. While holding the collar (gently!), allow the lead to fall to the floor and stand on it right beside your dog's front paw, hanging on to the handle all the while.
3. Now you can let go of the collar, straighten up, and keep holding on to that handle. A 6-foot lead is ideal for this.
4. Ignore your dog. No more interaction between you.

Your dog can take any position she likes. She's simply unable to pull or jump up. Your hands are free to delve into your purse or drink a coffee. Passers-by are safe from being jumped on. Your dog will find that as nothing more is happening, sitting or lying down is a good option. Your anxious dog can relax, knowing that nothing more is expected of her.

When you get fluent and quick at parking, you'll have a way to anchor your dog easily. Be sure to hold the collar before trying to stand on the lead or you'll find yourself doing the can-can as your dog flies forward as you try to get your foot on a waving lead!

Keeping your hands soft

Keeping your hands soft on a floppy lead can be hard to do. You've spent ages holding the lead tight as if your life depended on it, restricting your dog's freedom. This is understandable as you may have been afraid he would hurt someone.

But now we want the dog to have freedom - freedom to choose to stay calm! - so making sure you keep your hands soft and the lead loose is going to go a long way towards this. If your dog sails off away from you, you need to be able to stop him without yanking him off his feet. You want him to slow down, turn, and choose to come back to you. The lead needs to stay fluid so nothing sudden happens. Your anxious grasp when you clutch the lead tight and the tension this causes will tell your dog that something bad is happening. Perhaps he'd better bark at the nearest thing to keep it away!

I know you're thinking that if you loosen the lead, he'll pull all the time - but that's the old thinking. You now know that giving your dog the freedom to choose and then rewarding the choice you want will have him making good decisions in no time. As he learns these new skills, things will be changing dramatically before your eyes. Remember to choose a quiet area to practice - you can't teach these new skills in the middle of the park or a busy shopping street!

Holding the handle safely and flaking the line

Whatever lead you are using (and please don't use one less than 6 feet in length!) you need to hold it safely. Safe so that your hand can't slip out, and safe so that your wrist can't get broken if your dog suddenly lurches out at an angle. I am right-handed and have given the instructions for a right-hander. Use whichever hand feels comfortable for you.

Key Lead Skill No.3a
Holding the handle safely

1. Hold the lead handle up in one hand - say, your left hand - while the other hand - your right hand - goes through the loop like threading a needle
2. Then, while the handle is round your right wrist, bring the lead up and grip it against your right hand with your right thumb.
3. The line is now emerging from between your thumb and hand. This way you have a secure hold without stress, and your bones are safe!
4. Your other hand will be a channel for the line to run through loosely to your dog.

If this has totally confused you (sorry), you will be pleased to know that there is a video illustrating this and the following lead skills which you'll find in the Resources section.

Long line skills

For a lot of the training you'll be learning, you'll need to use a long line. Panic not! It's very easy when you know how. I find that people - once introduced to the joys of the long line - never want to go back to a short lead, except, of course, on the street.

This long line is not going to trail on the ground - it's going to stay in your hands, free of mud and wet, and is not going to wind your dog's legs up in knots or be a trip hazard for you or any passing children. You can watch the video in the Resources section, and I'll describe it for you here too.

A long line of about 15 feet is perfect for our purposes - see Chapter 1 of this book. It will provide a connection between you and your dog while allowing her to mooch around in a natural manner, and - importantly - give her the freedom to express her body language. You will always have a safe hold of the handle (and a lot of the line) but you can allow your dog to make choices. Don't worry, we'll make sure these are all good choices! Just like the red or blue jumper offered to your toddler, we will limit the range of choices she can make, and weight the best choice heavily in our favour.

So the first thing to learn is how to control that line without breaking your fingers, or causing your dog to be yanked to a halt. This system is known by the nautical term "flaking" - used when the line is laid out on the deck in figures of eight, or snaked. This ensures that when the net is thrown overboard, the line runs freely and there is no danger of a knot stopping the net from deploying, or of a coil catching a sailor's leg and taking him overboard with it.

You may be in the habit of winding a rope up in loose coils. The danger of this is that if your dog suddenly shoots forward, a coil will close round your fingers. There is a very real danger of breaking a finger this way!

Key Lead Skill No.3b
Flaking the line

1. Layer your line, in the hand holding the handle, in long bows or figures of eight.
2. As your dog moves away, you can open your fingers for the line to snake out through the channel your other hand is making, then as you and your dog near each other again,
3. you can flake it into your hand again so it's not touching the ground.

All these lead skills really become very easy with a bit of practice - even for people who have difficulty distinguishing left and right, or who are not very nimble-handed. The long line will become a soft and relaxed connection between you and your dog. It will shrink and grow organically as your dog moves closer to you then further away again. It's like gently holding a child's hand, rather than gripping that hand tight as you might if you were near a busy road with a fractious four-year-old.

Whoa there!

So let's look now at how you can slow your dog to a gentle halt without pulling. You really never have to pull your dog's lead again!

Key Lead Skill No. 4
Slow Stop

1. Your dog is heading away from you, perhaps in pursuit of a good scent, or trying to reach someone.
2. As he moves away, loosely cup your left hand under the lead, letting the line run through freely, gradually closing your grip so he can feel this squeezing action as the lead slows down.
3. This will slow him sufficiently to ease him into a stand.
4. Now relax your hands and lead - you may need to take a small step forward to let your hands soften and drop down - and admire your dog standing on a loose lead.
5. You can attract him back to your side if you need to with your voice - treat, and carry on.

This should all be calm, mostly noiseless, and easy. It's like holding your friend's hand and gently slowing them down till they come back into step beside you. No need for "Oi!" "Stop!" "C'me 'ere" or anything else other than saying, "Good Boy!" and giving him a welcoming smile when he reorients to you.

Try this first with another person instead of your dog to help you. Ask them to hold the clip of the lead in their hand, turn away from you and let the lead drape over their shoulder, with you behind them holding the line. As they walk away and you start to close the fingers of your left hand on the lead, they should be fully aware of that sensation and respond to it. They'll be able to tell you very clearly if you're gently slowing them or jolting them to a stop! Your dog too will recognise this feeling on the lead as "Oh hallo, we're stopping now."

When you start, it may take a few attempts to get your dog to stay still and balanced when she stops so that you're able to relax the lead. After a while she'll know that this rubbing sensation on the lead is the precursor to a halt. The right sort of harness will help enormously to get her to balance on her own four feet instead of using you as a fifth leg. See the Resources section at the end of the book.

You may find that your dog slows beautifully to a halt, but as soon as you relax your line she surges forward again! So when you slow stop her, relax your hands just a little (an inch or so) to test whether she's standing balanced on her own feet. If she immediately starts to lean forward again, don't move, but ease her to a stop again - maybe just using your fingers on the line - and test again. Sooner or later, she's going to realise that slow stop means stand still. The point to remember is that if you've decided she should stop (you may be seeing trouble up ahead) then stop she shall. Don't move yourself once you've committed to stopping.

But what if stopping is not enough?

There are going to be times when you can slow stop your dog, but she is still trying to surge forward. Maybe you're just too close to the thing that's worrying her. So, as you know from Chapter 3 of this book:

Whenever your dog is unhappy about a situation, the first thing to do is make distance.

But how can you do that? You know that if you try and haul her back when she's this aroused that it's going to turn into an ugly mess. Not only is it hard to drag her backwards - her feet are firmly planted behind her and you're pulling against her strongest muscles, in her back and haunches (think of a horse drawing a cart) - but worse, just trying to pull her back may trigger an outburst.

You are going to love this lead skill! Instead of trying to force her to comply with what you want, remember the red and blue jumpers: give her a choice!

Always allow time for a choice

Key Lead Skill No.5
Stroking the line

1. Hold onto the line and stay put yourself to make sure your dog can't move forward
2. With a hand-over-hand action, *gently stroke* the line as you make attractive cooing and kissy noises (you are *not* pulling the lead).
3. Your dog will feel this feathery touch and turn to look at you, as you bend over behind her in a kind of play-bow inviting her to join you.
4. She'll turn of her own volition and trot happily towards you, the scary thing quite forgotten.
5. Back up a few steps while she engages her eyes with yours, then you can turn and head away.

It's as easy as that. It is a joy! And people are usually astonished when they learn this skill. Make sure you have the other skills down before you start on this one.

Most of you will have some experience with children, either through having your own, or through having been one. Think of the times you've wanted to distract your child - possibly from a dangerous situation - by saying "Is that a *giraffe* over there?" or some such. You get a lightning response! This is the same kind of idea we're using here. Distraction and diversion and a lightness of voice.

All these lead skills can be done with a short or a long line. I find that it's easier to learn the first two on a short line, and the next three on a long line. Once you've mastered them, you can use them with any lead.

It's you who has to do some learning here. Just like driving a car, if you grate the gears and stamp on the pedals your car is not going to perform well. To get a smooth "drive" with your dog, you're going to need to learn these Key Lead Skills carefully. Your dog will say, "Oh, that's what she wants!" and it will all become a breeze. You really will wonder how you managed before!

In this chapter we've learnt that

- The lead is a lovesome thing that forms a connection between you and your dog
- There's no need to haul your dog about
- You never have to pull your dog's lead again!
- Choice is the name of the game

Section 2

Choice Training

Chapter 5
Why Choice Training?

As we've seen, Choice Training is empowering to dogs. It's empowering to people too, and is the more enlightened way to educate children, both at home and at school. If you can involve the subject in their own education/training, they have the ability to decide things for themselves instead of having things done *to* them.

You may be thinking that if you give your dog a choice she'll automatically choose the wrong one. But that's where a bit of clever setting up can help weight her choices in our favour. Remember those red and blue jumpers, where you didn't care which one was chosen, but you didn't offer the fairy outfit?

Choice Training is the method used for successful training of guide dogs for the blind, seizure alert dogs, dogs for the disabled, search and rescue dogs, dogs for PTSD sufferers, and the like. Even police dogs are now beginning to be trained in a humane way that honours the dog, and there are some notable trailblazers in this field (see the Appreciation page).

Not only can dogs learn these useful skills to help mankind, but they can do them for the sheer enjoyment! Take dancing with dogs, dog tricks, dressage for dogs (aka Obedience competition), agility, flyball, not to mention picking things up for you at home, fetching the lead, finding your phone …

Then there are the truly astonishing feats! Not only have dogs been taught to drive a car, but they have also flown a plane in tricky manoeuvres. See the

Resources section if you don't believe me! Watch some of the footage of these achievements - using abandoned dogs from shelters - and you'll never dismiss your dog's intelligence again! All this is done fastest with Choice Training.

Handling

Many reactive dogs are sensitive in other areas too. So touch sensitivity and sound sensitivity may need to be addressed.

ACTION STEP 19:

Revisit the **Collar Hold game**, featured in Book 1 and again in Chapter 1 of this book. It's fundamental that you should be able to slide a hand easily into your dog's collar and achieve connection and calm. If you haven't done this exercise yet, *do it now!*

Treating touch sensitivity is a similar process - light touch, feed treat; light touch, feed treat - as you touch different parts of your dog's body, using different pressure (sometimes a feather touch, sometimes a press, sometimes a soft squeeze, e.g. of the paw). Be sure that you are not holding the treat to the dog's nose *while* you touch him. If you do that he will be focussed so closely on the treat that he may not even notice you touching him - which defeats the object of the exercise! We want him to be fully aware, but tolerant and not fearful. The essence of this method is to work in short sessions (maybe one minute long) and only very gradually up the ante. You don't leap from a soft touch of the face into a close examination of his back teeth!

If a particular spot is a no-go area for your dog, go and get that thorough vet check! If there's intermittent buried pain your vet may struggle to locate it in a dog who is tense and anxious under examination and not giving anything away. This is where you will have success with a canine massage therapist who can relax the dog before delving into their bodies. See Book 1, and the Resources section. *I'd* be snappy if anyone touching *me* sparked off a searing pain.

Remember that an abnormally aggressive response to touch, especially in a sleeping dog, needs a thorough vet check for pain or other neurological cause.

Is it you that's causing the pain?

The key here is that your dog will associate *something* with any pain or discomfort he's feeling. That something he's latched on to may be the approach of a person holding a broom. It may be entering the vet's surgery. It may be being manhandled so you can reach his claws. So if you have to administer a treatment which may be uncomfortable, it's a good idea to get him to associate something else with this pain, and not you!

There are various techniques about that focus on the dog giving you permission to treat him - having him become a party to his own treatment. Picture this: you go to the dentist for your appointment. While you're talking to the receptionist, the dentist creeps up on you, grabs your jaw and forces it open to poke instruments in. Horror! This is an assault! And yet isn't this what people often do to their dogs?

A better scenario would be that you go into the dentist's surgery. He indicates *The Chair*. Now when you get into that chair you are effectively giving the dentist permission to open your mouth and start poking about in there. It's just as unpleasant as before - but this time you gave your consent.

So get your dog to give you consent by transferring the "this may hurt" feelings onto something else. Some people use a pot of treats on the floor. As long as the dog sits or lies still in front of that pot he'll be given a treat. Gradually you can pick up a paw or start brushing a tail while you dish out the treats. If your dog leaps up and flees, let him. When he ventures back he can choose to station himself in front of the treat pot again. He's saying, "Ok, you can brush me now". You could also get out the implements he's worried about - the nail clippers or the claw-grinder, and perhaps use a particular mat for him to sit on, which you only use for treatments. When he comes to you, you can reward him for his bravery. He knows what's going to happen - you're not going to jump him.

If you call your dog over for a cuddle then grab him and swing him over onto his back so you can check his tangles, how's he going to feel next time you call him?

Choice, choice, choice! Think of that dentist and let your dog have a say in his own care.

That's my name!

The biggest area of conflict around choice may well be the recall. Your dog is off gallivanting about, rolling in who-knows-what, playing with other dogs or chasing a bunny trail, and you call him. Now he has a choice! Does he ignore you, or come barrelling in to you just to experience your delight with him? The recall warrants a whole book to itself, and in fact it has one - the fourth book in the series **Essential Skills for a Brilliant Family Dog**: *Here Boy! Step-by-step to a Stunning Recall from your Brilliant Family Dog*. More info in the Resources section.

But you can make a start, right there where you're reading this. Say your dog's name. Did he perk up, open his eyes, prick his ears, give a slow thud of his tail, even come over to you? Any of those responses is a good one and warrants a treat. Be sure you only ever use your dog's name when you can pair it with something good (see **Lesson 1: The Precious Name Game** in Book 1). I'll show you again here, as it's critically important that your dog thinks his name is wonderful and always worth responding to. We expect a lot — we need to build in the response we want before taking it for granted.

ACTION STEP 20:

Lesson 1: The Precious Name Game revisited

1. Say dog's name cheerily whenever you notice him
2. When he responds - by raising an eyebrow or hurtling towards you and crashing into your legs - reward him with something good
3. Repeat at every opportunity throughout the day
4. Enjoy your dog

Your reward may be a treat, putting his lead on for a walk (if walks are enjoyable), opening the door to the garden, playing a game, and so on.

In this chapter we have learnt that:

- Giving your dog a choice will result in better decisions from her
- You can extend this choice-making to letting her participate in her own care
- Her first choice should be to respond automatically to her name

Chapter 6
Is this all woolly ideas or is there real science behind it?

If facts and figures are anathema to you, skip to the next chapter. But if the nuts and bolts of human and animal behaviour interest you - why we actually do what we do - then read on. References are in the Resources section.

Looking first at specifically dog-focussed scientific work, the two pillars are Pavlov, the originator of Classical Conditioning, and B.F. Skinner, whose pioneering work with a broad range of animals resulted in Operant Conditioning being shown to be the best way to train any animal. We're animals too.

Pavlov's Dogs and Classical Conditioning

Classical Conditioning was first described by Ivan Pavlov (1849-1936). This area of study came as a by-product of his pioneering work on the human digestive system for which he won a Nobel Prize in 1904. His work was far-reaching and forms the basis of what we know about digestion today.

But his name has been linked in the popular mind with one thing only – Pavlov's Dogs. In his study of the purpose and function of saliva, Pavlov used dogs in his laboratory. They were kept immobile, with drains collecting the saliva through fistulae in the dogs' necks. The objective was to collect the saliva for analysis when the dogs were fed. It was soon discovered, however, that the dogs would begin salivating increasingly earlier in the food preparation chain - first the sight of the lab technicians, then just the sound of human activity, became enough to get the juices flowing in anticipation of their food.

Pavlov's genius was in interrupting this chain with a specific, non-food-linked sound. Amongst others, he chose his famous bell. The bell was rung before feeding, and after a few exposures, the dogs would begin to salivate at the sound of the bell - regardless of the time or other factors – and in the absence of food. Pavlov had effectively put the salivation (an unconditioned or spontaneous, unconsidered response) under stimulus control. Put another way, the bell cued the drooling. So by using a hitherto neutral stimulus (the bell) he could cause the salivation to occur without the normal, natural, unconditioned stimulus of the presence of food. The association that the bell signified food meant the bell would cue the drooling in the absence of food.

How does this apply to us?

With your own dog, you'll be able to see many examples of Classical Conditioning at work:

- Barking at the doorbell
- Leaping up at the sound of the car keys or when seeing you pick up the lead
- Appearing at your feet when you bang the dog bowl
- Rapt attention at the sound of the fridge door opening,
- or a plastic bag rustling,
- or the cat flap opening!

These sights or sounds all stimulate a response of excitement or salivation, even without the expected result of a visitor at the door, going for a walk, dinner, or the entry of the cat. This response has developed through continual repetition of a sequence which the dog now anticipates.

You can see now where some of your dog's more annoying habits have come from, and how you can change them! Control the stimulus (the thing that's causing the reaction) and you control the outcome. In fact, if you remove the stimulus entirely - disconnect the doorbell, for instance - you can completely eliminate that response. Think about that!

Operant Conditioning

Operant Conditioning is the name given to the shaping system first described by B.F. Skinner (1904-1990) in 1938 in *The Behavior of Organisms.*

Skinner was influenced by Pavlov. Working largely with rats and pigeons, Skinner's work had a far-reaching effect on education and psychology. From a practical standpoint, it was used extensively in the American war effort in the forties. Dolphins were used for underwater work where it was unsafe for divers, and chickens became ace spotters - of life rafts in a choppy ocean far below the rescue plane - and of bombing targets.

It was developed and refined by the dolphin trainers who, after World War II, turned their attention to training animals for aquarium displays. The dolphin trainers introduced a marker. It's impossible to get a fish to a dolphin at the high point of a jump, so they marked the moment with a whistle, signalling the correct response from the animal and the imminent arrival of a fish. This whistle is a Secondary Reinforcer.

- A Primary Reinforcer is something that the subject finds innately reinforcing, such as food, play, or social interaction.

- A Secondary Reinforcer is found rewarding by the subject by its association with a Primary Reinforcer, for example money, tokens, whistle, clicker, or a marker word - "Yes!"

Operant Conditioning is so called because the subject has to decide to do something to achieve a reward - to operate on its environment. In Classical

Conditioning, an action which occurs naturally is paired with a stimulus or cue. For example, offering your hand for the dog to touch: the dog comes to sniff your hand, then you add the cue to the hand-touching action. This cue could be a word, or simply offering your hand. In Operant Conditioning the animal can make a choice of what behaviour to offer.

In a "Skinner Box" - a small chamber for testing the responses of animals, often equipped with a food-producing mechanism - rats or pigeons could sleep, groom, run around, or press a lever which delivered food - a Primary Reinforcer. Skinner introduced Pavlov's discoveries by pairing a stimulus to the food delivery, so the subjects knew that touching the lever produced food. Naturally, touching the lever became very popular! When Skinner stopped rewarding the lever-pressing by failing to deliver food, after a flurry of repeated attempts and frustration the action died out entirely – that's known as an Extinction Burst.

Picture the angry toddler demanding an ice cream: he will get louder and noisier until (if unrewarded) … eventually he gives up.

Why does this matter to me and my pet dog?

The possibilities opened up by Operant Conditioning extend far beyond simply achieving a desired action. It has become a window into the animal's mind. Daily, we are extending our knowledge of how the critters think. The practical applications are boundless: in dogs alone we have mine detection, search and rescue, dogs for the disabled, hearing dogs for the deaf, seeing dogs for the blind, seizure alert medical assistance dogs, companion dogs, entertaining dogs, dancing dogs, agility dogs. A lot of the things these dogs can do would be very difficult, if not impossible, to teach by force, by luring, or by moulding the action - and there would be no enthusiasm and joy in the task!

Skinner's pioneering work, followed up and expanded by Marion Breland, Bob Bailey, and Karen Pryor amongst others, has enabled dogs to be used in so many of these new applications.

The important thing to remember with Operant Conditioning is that what you reinforce is what you get, so the timing of the reward is crucial! One moment you think you are capturing a wonderful Sit Pretty, but because you were too slow with your marker, you actually reinforced a floppy Sit. Remember the dolphins jumping: your marker means a reward is on its way. Clarity is key!

A word about punishment

Operant Conditioning has its own clearly defined language - Reinforcement or Punishment, Positive or Negative - which can confuse people as it may not mean the same as is popularly perceived.

- Positive means adding or starting something
- Negative means taking something away or stopping it
- Reinforcement means to encourage what you want by rewarding it, making it more likely to happen again
- Punishment refers to punishing the behaviour, not the animal, making the action less likely to happen again. It does not necessarily include traditional punishments such as beating.

Put very briefly:

- Positive Reinforcement = Good starts
- Positive Punishment = Bad starts
- Negative Reinforcement = Bad stops
- Negative Punishment = Good stops

These are known as the Four Quadrants.

But you don't need to remember all this - *just aim for Positive Reinforcement and reward what you like!*

If your dog does something you like, for instance, and you turn away and ignore her, this is punishing - discouraging the action. Imagine walking down the street, spotting someone you know, giving a cheery smile, and your acquaintance turns his head sharply away to walk past you without a word. How would you feel? What would you do next time you saw him on the street?

Skinner proved that if an action is rewarded, the subject is likely to repeat that action. Similarly, if an action is punished, the subject is unlikely to repeat it. How many times did you have to put your hand into the steam from a kettle before you stopped doing it? There is fallout from punishment, however, that eliminates its use from any humane training program. Obviously it causes unhappiness and pain, which should render it unacceptable to civilised people, but it also causes distrust, alienation, lying, and deceitful behaviour. If a child has been smacked for stealing a cake, he's going to make very sure he doesn't get caught while stealing the next one! It doesn't necessarily stop what you don't want - it may drive it underground.

Repeatedly rewarding what you *do* like will work much, much faster, and your dog's response will be durable - she'll always make the right choice. It is the element of choice that will transform your relationship with your dog, and - secret tip! - it works just the same with children, spouses, and work colleagues!

Think of the joy of never administering a telling-off ever again!

Impulse Control

There is plenty of scientific proof concerning the principles of instant versus delayed gratification in humans, and it appears to me that it works just the same in your dog.

Sigmund Freud, back in 1911, argued that deferred gratification was a marker of increased maturity. Then Walter Mischel conducted his Marshmallow Test experiments at Stanford University in the late 1960s, on children between ages three and five. In the Marshmallow Test, a child had to choose between eating one favourite treat straight away, or - if they could wait for 15 minutes - be rewarded with two treats. A small number of the children caved in straight away and settled for one treat. Of the remainder who chose to wait, only one third managed to last out the fifteen minutes and earn their double reward.

One of the findings was that if the researcher interacting with the child appeared inconsistent and broke promises, the child would lose faith in the new game and just take his one marshmallow while he could. This provides an interesting insight into our need as parents and dog-owners to be consistent and reliable - however busy or stressed we may be!

The detailed follow-up studies over the next 40 years were revealing. The children who, at 4, were able to delay gratification did better in school and university, were more successful, and enjoyed a more healthy lifestyle. The ability to make good choices is a predictor of a person's ability to make the best of their life. They can choose rational behaviour over desires - the pre-frontal cortex over the limbic system.

Cognitive Behavioural Therapy uses the "if-then" framework to help people overcome unwanted desires. "If this happens, then I move into that strategy." Repetition leads to new habits being formed.

So while the ability to control impulses in the face of food does not directly impinge on your dog's fearfulness, it is something that he can apply to the actions he takes, and will hugely help him to move into strategies that will work for him in the future. Essentially, dogs do what works. And we are going to give him techniques that will work better than his current knee-jerk reaction of barking and lunging at something he fears.

How empowering this is for your dog!

In this Chapter you've learnt that:

- The research into the dog's mind is very advanced
- How you can adapt this knowledge for you and your pet
- People and dogs are much the same
- "It's all Greek to me," says your dog

Chapter 7
An introduction to Choice Training

Let's get into how Choice Training works.

1. Catch your dog doing something right

If you are ignoring your dog when he's quiet and affable, and as soon as he puts a paw out of line you come down on him like a ton of bricks, you are teaching him to focus on the thing you don't like. And all the time he was doing something you *do* like, it was not being noted or admired!

You want to switch this around. Your training mantra (which I gave you in Book 1) is:

Reward what you like
Ignore what you don't like
Manage what you can't ignore

To begin with, you may find this very hard! But this slots very well into All-Day Training. Rather than having formal training sessions with your dog, regard every interaction as a training session. You don't want your dog to *perform on cue*, so much as just be. And his just being is what you want to focus on.

If you don't give him a choice, it'll be pot luck whether he ever works out what you want. Giving him a choice, showing him that his actions affect outcomes, gives him a responsibility that he will grow into. This will change your relationship for both of you. Rather than a master-robot relationship, you will have a friend-companion relationship. Much easier, much calmer, and much more fun!

Examples:

a) Your dog is jumping up on you. You yell "Down!" and flap your hands (this is a great reward for jumping). Dog carries on jumping.

Alternative using your mantra:

Your dog is jumping up on you. You turn away and imagine you can see no dog. Dog ceases jumping and waits for you to come back. Now you can reward him for not jumping!

You are focussing on your dog keeping his feet on the floor

b) Your dog is jumping up on a visitor. You yell "Down!" while your visitor flaps his hands and laughs, saying, "I don't mind" (He does. He really does mind.)

Alternative using your mantra:

You have your dog on a lead before your visitor arrives. You park him (see Key Lead Skill No.2 in Chapter 4 of this book). When he is calm he gets given permission to "Go say Hi", and comes straight back to you for his reward.

You are focussing on your dog greeting calmly

c) Your dog raids the kitchen bin. There is rubbish everywhere. You tell him off, focussing on the mess on the floor. He may think you're just cross and it has nothing to do with him. Or he may think that next time he raids the bin he'll make sure to make himself scarce when you come home. (This is not shame or guilt, just fear.)

Alternative using your mantra:

Your dog raids the kitchen bin. You realise your mistake in leaving him and the bin together unattended. You greet him warmly as usual, clear up the mess without comment and put the bin safely out of his reach. Be sure to leave your dog something he *is* allowed to rip or chew next time you leave him.

You are focussing on your dog's needs, not your own convenience

Focus on what you want, not what you don't want!

What you focus on is what you get.

2. Marker Training

To make sure your dog knows exactly what it is you like, you can mark the split-second she's doing it. You can use your voice - useful as you always have your voice with you. You need to make your marker very short and snappy. "Yes!" is a popular choice. If you say "Good girl" you're likely to spin these words out slowly - "Goooood girrrrrrrl" - so that by the time you've said it your dog is on to something else. You are no longer marking a smart sit, but a shuffle of the paws and a gaze out of the window.

You can also use a clicker. This has the advantage of always sounding the same, so different people can make the exact same marker when they train the dog with it. It doesn't express emotion, so you don't burden your dog with your disappointment or frustration. This can be a plus or a minus. It's nice to be able to inject some enthusiasm into your training with your voice when you need to jizz things up a bit.

You can use either or both. The principle of marking accurately what you like - the moment your dog does it - is the same.

So also is the fact that Marker = Reward. If you mark, with a word or a click, you must now reward your dog. That's the deal you cut with her. If you spoke or clicked by mistake, it doesn't matter - you still reward your dog. You can quickly undo your mistake with a couple of accurate clicks or Yeses.

Once your dog twigs that if she can get you to say Yes, or to click, a reward is guaranteed, you'll suddenly find you have a willing learner who is ready to try things to see what works.

When you want to lead up your dog, for example, instead of chasing her round the kitchen or fighting her off your chest, you can simply stand still holding the lead. Lead = walk = excitement, so your dog will be bouncing around. Now you wait. Wait till she has four feet on the ground, mark with a Yes, and clip the lead on - the going out for a walk is the reward.

You can be imaginative with your rewards! Remember, a reward is something *your dog* finds rewarding, not something you think she ought to like.

But just before we launch into Rewards, I'll mention the No-Reward Marker. This is what you can use to indicate to your dog that she has been unsuccessful and no reward is forthcoming. Please use this very very sparingly or - better still - not at all. You can end up using your words as power steering as you say "Yes. Ah-ah. Nooooooo. Yes. No. Oh no." etc. Your dog is no longer truly making choices, just trying things and seeing whether you respond with a yes (treat) or a No-Reward Marker. It can make your dog very anxious as they really have little idea what it is you want, and can cause them to give up entirely. The only time I may use it is by saying a sad "Oh?" to encourage a re-think.

You can add a Keep Going Signal by way of encouragement. "You've nearly got it - Yes, that's it!" or "Where should you be now? What about your feet? Yes!" I know my dog does not understand the words, but she gets my meaning and tries harder.

It's essential that she's free to try things that don't work, thus finding what does work.

3. Rewards

"Hmm – looks like a training game is coming!"

Let's look at what you need to make sure your dog loves this new choice game!

1. A selection of toys your dog absolutely loves. Balls on ropes; soft tug toys made of fleece, sheepskin, or rabbit skin; and teddy bear-type toys, are all good. Squeaky toys may cause your dog to lose his mind and may not be much use in a training session.

2. Mega-desirable treats! This means treats that your dog will sell her soul for, not dry kibble or pocket fluff. You can get some first-class commercial treats if you hunt carefully, but the best treats tend to be home-prepared, soft, slippery, flavoursome, smelly, and small. Revisit the Rewards section in Chapter 2 of this book, and fill your fridge and your pockets with irresistible goodies. (If you live in a hot country you'll probably want to use a treat-bag, not your pocket!)

If you asked me to run an errand for you, then said, "Here's a lovely bowl of oranges for you as a thank you," I'd be unimpressed. I hate oranges. If you offered me a dry biscuit, that would be so-so, and I may decline it and head away. Now if you were to say "Would you like a piece of chocolate cake?" that would be another matter entirely! I'd be saying, "Is there anything else you'd like me to do?"

So be sure the treats you're offering are worth working for, exactly match your dog's individual preferences, and desirable enough to distract your reactive dog when she's under pressure.

How many rewards should I give?

Don't get hung up over treats: they are a means to an end. You get paid for going to work - why shouldn't your dog? So how many treats should you give? Whatever it takes! I aim to dish out a lot of treats to my crew every day. But they only get a treat when they do something I like. So that means the more things they do that I like, the more treats will come. They get that!

And I don't distinguish between doing and not doing - for instance, stopping barking and not starting barking. Both are rewardable. When my barky dog gets a reward for stopping barking, the others (who may or may not have joined in) get a treat for their silence.

One thing you may find is that kibble or relatively uninteresting treats can work better if you are working on - for example, resting on a mat. Using ultra-exciting treats, speaking excitedly, using a clicker, can all work against you in this situation. So there is a place for lower-value treats - thus saving the heavy artillery for when you're out in the thick of it!

Keep in mind that the ability to take food is a clear signal of your dog's mental state. If she's unable to take treats she normally loves - it's time to make distance! (See Chapter 3 of this book.)

Homework sessions

A word about length of sessions. As suggested above, a lot of your dog's learning will be on-the-go - you'll be catching moments that please you and rewarding them. This may spread into a short practice session for one of the exercises here. But when you have a formal training session, that too should be as short as possible. I aim to work for maybe 60 seconds - and that will include play - or about 10-20 treats. The sessions are very intensive but very short and usually exciting. Nobody has time to get bored!

When you're working outside your sessions will be longer, but only long enough! I'll be showing you how to judge that later on.

4. Pattern Games

This is a name first coined by Leslie McDevitt (see Resources section) for her excellent games designed to help anxious dogs. They are simplicity itself, and their success depends on establishing a quick, light, rhythm. Only one action is required from your dog, and that is marked and rewarded.

Dogs learn by rhythm and patterning (as do we), and these games are a fun way to get what you want very quickly. They can be played anywhere, though it's best to start indoors in a place your dog feels comfortable. For me, that's our small kitchen.

I'm going to give you three pattern games inspired by Leslie McDevitt that will help you to get fast engagement from your dog. Once they know the games well (and they love them), you'll be able to use them as a way to settle your dog in a difficult situation. As long as you are far enough away from his trigger, you can start playing one of these games and get total involvement and joy in the game. The worries your dog had will evaporate as he feels the security and pleasure of playing with you.

Lesson 3: The Focus Game

1. Stand and place a treat on the floor to the right of your foot. Your dog will eat it and possibly sniff about for more. Finding none, she'll look towards you to see if any more treats are coming.

2. Say "YES!" enthusiastically the second she turns to you and place another treat - quickly and with a flourish - to your left.

3. As your dog looks up from eating it, say "YES!" and place another treat to your right, and so on, getting into a fast rhythmic dance.

Once your dog knows the game you'll be able to throw the treat to right or left without having to bend over and place it. It's not a game of "Hunt the Treat," so be sure your dog sees where you drop it so she can grab it instantly and turn. A bowling action is better than a toss as your piece of cheese will land who-knows-where if you toss it.

It may take several short sessions before your dog is keen to run back and forth in front of you like a pendulum. This may take days - don't worry about a timetable. She's learning to focus on you, turning quickly to look at you after grabbing her treat. Repeat the Focus Game till it becomes totally automatic and slick for both of you - and always ends up with smiles from you and that zany expression on your dog's face. Say "All done," and toss her a toy.

Lesson 4: The Name Game

Now we can move forward to the Name Game. Here, we will establish that your dog's name means a fast head-turn.

1. Start with the Focus Game and, once you have a rhythm, add your dog's name *just as she's diving* for the treat. She has time only to grab it and turn.

2. Say "YES!" exactly as her head turns. You are marking the muscle movement in the neck (just like athletes train accuracy).

3. Repeat now till your dog is spinning round, ears flapping, just after you've said her name, and turning with joy and enthusiasm!

4. Stop while you're ahead! About ten treats or a minute or so is enough.

Watchpoint

Be sure you say your dog's name just as she's about to grab the treat then follow with "Yes!" for the head-turn, then toss the treat. The sequence is

(toss treat)
Name
Yes!
Treat
Name
Yes!
Treat ...

Develop a rhythm and make sure these are separate events. Keep your hands together till after you've said Yes, then you can deliver the treat. Don't let all the steps happen at once or confusion will reign!

Lesson 5: The Sit Game

You need to have a firm rhythm established in your Focus Game before embarking on the Sit Game. You're going to break the rhythm in order to move the goalposts, so you have to have a rhythm so that you can break it!

1. Start with your Focus Game until you're both in the groove
2. After a few Yeses and treats, this time when your dog looks at you, *say nothing*
3. She'll likely stare at you and say "I'm looking at you - where's my treat?" Keep waiting
4. She may jump up at you, she may bark at you. Make no response and keep waiting
5. Eventually she will sit. Hurrah! "Yes!" Treat! Toss the treat away from her so she has to get up
6. Repeat from 5 till her sits are quick and fluent.
7. Add the word "Sit" as her bottom is heading for the floor (don't wait till she's sat).

In one short session, or possibly two, your dog has learnt to sit when nothing else is asked of her. You have labelled it as "Sit". And nowhere did you tell your dog to do anything! This is the essence of Choice Training. She worked it out all by herself.

Watchpoint

If you get to step 3 and your dog gets anxious because you're saying nothing, be sure to keep her in the game *without helping her*. So you may smile, relax your stance, you may quietly say, "How are you going to get this treat, then?"

If seconds are passing and your dog is frozen to the spot and getting worried, just go back to the Focus Game for a few treats so she knows she's doing the right thing, then try again. Sooner or later she'll stop worrying and start thinking. This response is not uncommon in a dog who responds to everything with anxiety, or who has always been told what to do in the past. No longer! She's going to learn to stand on her own four feet.

ACTION STEP 21:

Be sure to play these games daily, for just a few treats. Remember training sessions should be very brief and often spontaneous. My dogs know that if I head for the coffee machine there's a good chance of a game or two while coffee is being made. Kettle time is a good time - grab a handful of treats and in the minute it takes your kettle to boil you have done a chunk of training with your dog! While all three games build your dog's confidence, the Name Game is obviously a winner when it comes to building your Stunning Recall (see Resources section).

In this chapter, we have learnt that:

- Choice Training builds your dog's confidence and independence
- It enables your dog to explore his huge capabilities
- Pattern games are very satisfying and a quick way to teach key concepts
- The sky's the limit!

Section 3

Relaxation and Walk Management

Chapter 8
Three essentials for safe walks

1. Impulse Control

This has been mentioned a number of times. Because it's essential! You can't teach a child who is continually trying to do something else because of lack of focus and an attraction to shiny objects (or anything that moves or is edible). The same goes for your dog.

And while the quickest and simplest way to teach your dog this skill is with food, its applications are not limited to food!

Think of:

- your dog calmly waiting for you to open the door till released to go out, then to sit and wait for you while you close the door
- the comfort and safety you'll enjoy doing the same trick with exits from the car
- respect for your furniture
- polite toy play which leaves your fingers intact
- your dog taking treats nicely and still leaving those fingers intact
- no more stealing! no more counter-surfing!
- walking past trees and lamp-posts without your dog hauling you over to check the pee-mail
- being able to pass exciting things without your dog becoming a hooligan

- seeing your dog become more thoughtful and reflective - fewer knee-jerk reactions!
- meeting and greeting politely

The opportunities are endless. All of these lead to a quiet life. When I've boarded individual dogs in my home in the past, I've always found it exhausting to be their impulse control for them. My dogs are not perfect (neither am I!) but life is so easy when you have a responsible dog around, and not a thieving chancer.

For a detailed program to teach your dog impulse control, see the second book in the series **Essential Skills for a Brilliant Family Dog** - *Leave it! How to teach Amazing Impulse Control to your Brilliant Family Dog* (see Resources Section) which you can get free after you get Book 1: *Calm Down!* also free. And if your dog is impetuous and his attention flittered, see the problem-solving e-course listed in the Resources section, which has lots of "recipes" to help you.

ACTION STEP 22:

Teach your dog impulse control. He's not going to learn without being shown. Hey - the book is free! Go get it!

---

2. Emergency Measures: protecting your dog

There are three quick ways to get your dog out of the line of fire when you're out.

Collar Hold

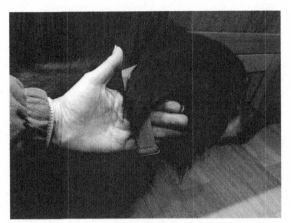

A soft touch on the neck tells Lacy to be still

I've shown you this game in Book 1 and again in Chapter 1 of this book. It's important! Not only are you able to immobilise your dog, and move her behind you as you turn in front of her, but the feel of the back of your hand resting against her neck will be calming to her. Putting your hand in your dog's collar is not a way of grabbing and hauling her about. It's that gentle connection we are always seeking.

Get behind

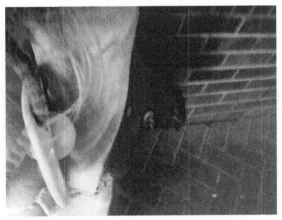

Lacy chooses to get behind

Very useful for giving your dog a hiding place. Teach her to run round you and peep out from behind your legs. One of the advantages of this is that your lead is now going behind your legs, so your dog will not be able to lurch forward. You can partially hide your dog this way, reducing the stimulus to the other dog, or the stranger advancing towards you intent on greeting your fearful dog.

Carwash (aka Middle)

I believe it was Grisha Stewart (Resources section) who chose this moniker! Similar to *Get behind* above, only your dog goes halfway round you and dives between your legs and sits. You can apply gentle pressure by squeezing your legs in - very comforting for some dogs. Carwash is particularly useful for people-fearful dogs. There are few people who will make so bold as to lean forward, advancing their hand towards your crotch, to bend over and touch your dog! Again, the lead is going round the back of your leg, so your dog can't pounce forward at the would-be greeter.

Lacy, if alarmed, may put herself into Carwash. She's telling me she's uncomfortable with the person or people nearby and needs a little reassurance that they won't try to interact with her. Lacy's catchphrase - borrowed from another glamour puss - is "I want to be alone"!

Lacy puts herself in Carwash

Lesson 6 Carwash

1. Have a treat in each hand and your dog facing you
2. Draw her round your right leg with the treat in your right hand
3. As she gets behind you, bring your left hand back to join your right hand between your spread legs and "take over" with that hand, drawing her forward between your legs
4. Encourage your dog to look up to your face, which will produce a sit
5. Repeat so your hand becomes a signal to send her round, with just a treat for sitting.
6. Once she loves this game, and bounces excitedly into position, you can name it "Carwash" (or whatever you like)

ACTION STEP 23:

Get all three of these emergency measures fluent. There's another one to come soon!

---

3. The muzzle

The first thing to do is to stop seeing the muzzle as a mark of shame.

Many years ago I read of a mother who had written to "Dear Abby" about her little boy who was deaf. She had such feelings of guilt and anxiety about this that she hated his hearing aids - the very thing she should have been glad of! This dislike was rubbing off onto her son, who was getting tricky about wearing them. The advice given was to give the hearing aids the honour and respect and gratitude they warranted. She was to lay out her son's clothes with the hearing aids proudly on the top of the pile. Fitting them to the child at the start of the day was to be an exciting moment of togetherness and hope.

This profound advice made a huge difference to the mother's outlook, and helped her son to cope with being different.

Revise your feelings about muzzles!

The primary purpose of the muzzle, of course, is to prevent anyone getting injured. If your dog has bitten or you feel is likely to bite, then you have a responsibility to protect others (however stupid you may think they are!). You can get muzzles in pretty colours, and even a black one will look cute adorned with ribbons or sparkly star stickers.

The very useful secondary aspect of muzzling your dog, however, is that it keeps people away! Hooray! Just what your anxious dog wants. People will cross the road to avoid this dog who they consider dangerous. Fact is, it's now the safest dog around, because of the muzzle!

You need to stop worrying about what other people think. It's really of little importance. There are other reasons for a dog to be muzzled apart from danger of biting, and keeping people away: maybe your dog eats stones or harvests other unsavoury and dangerous (read: costly vets' bills) things from the environment. Maybe she steals other dogs' toys and then challenges them to a duel. You don't have to apologise for your care and thoughtfulness. And keep in mind that it's worth teaching any dog to be happy with a muzzle. If an awkward or painful procedure is needed at the vet's, it's good if your dog is happy to wear her muzzle and is not subjected to the ignominy of being wrestled into one by strangers.

Be sure to use a basket muzzle, so your dog can pant, drink, bark, and eat treats without difficulty. And don't just buy a muzzle and whap it on her! You'll find a program to acclimatise your dog to the muzzle so that she's keen to put her face into it, in the Resources section.

In this chapter we have learnt that:

- Impulse Control will seep into every corner of your dog's life, and improve it
- You can use three quick fixes to move your dog out of trouble
- Muzzles are not the black beast - they're the white knight in shining armour!

Chapter 9
Relaxation, De-stress, and *Sleep*

The ability to switch off, to relax and restore, is much sought after by people with enormously busy schedules and responsibilities. The most successful build naps and quiet time into their day as a matter of course - and that downtime is inviolable! They have learnt its importance.

Teaching your dog how to switch off is essential to his mental wellbeing. Some dogs don't need to learn this! Cricket the Whippet is happy to spend 22 hours a day under a duvet, reserving her activity for mealtimes and short bursts of awe-inspiring speed. But she has an even temperament and no hang-ups over other dogs or people. Nothing even startles her!

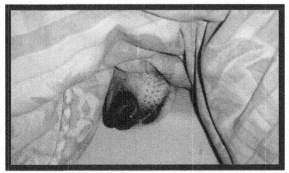

Sky the whippet under the duvet

But it's a sure bet that your reactive and anxious dog will keep pacing and worrying all day unless rest-time is enforced.

Relaxation and sleep

If ever a dog needed its rest and restorative sleep, it's the growly, fearful, or reactive dog. Think how you feel when you're short of sleep and have a challenging day ahead with the family, or at work! You start off on a short fuse, and that may get shorter as the day goes on.

Ensuring your dog gets enough downtime is critically important. It's often at the root of her troubles. Once she's getting enough restorative sleep she'll be better able to cope with all the trials and tribulations of life. As indicated in Book 1, dogs need a massive *17 hours of sleep a day* for optimal stresslessness. Is your dog getting anything like that? If not, you need to help him into a comfortable routine which does not involve endless pacing and activity.

Have a look at Tim, the rescue Border Collie, who I was visiting to work on his dog reactivity outside the house:

While I was there, it became clear that this hyperactive dog was wearing himself out. For the first twenty minutes of my visit he never stopped. He raced in and out of the room, jumped up my front, my back, chewed my hair, poked the other dog, ran off again, paced … never rested.

So I quickly amended my training plan to include some relaxation work straight away. After some active games to get Tim to engage with me, I started teaching him to slow down and relax. After just five minutes of this, his owner, expressed amazement at seeing her frantic dog actually lying down still for more than ten seconds at a time!

When I finished the short session and released him, what did he do? Do you think he went straight back into busybusy mode, panting and racing?

Nope. He just slid onto the floor beside us, and as he lay there his head started to loll, his eyelids drooped, and he was ... asleep! To the total astonishment of his owner, who had never seen him sleep in the day.

Want to know what I did to achieve this blissful calm state? See the first book in the **Essential Skills for a Brilliant Family Dog** series: *Calm Down! Step-by-Step to a Calm, Relaxed, and Brilliant Family Dog*, free at all e-book stores, to get the exact program. Quite apart from the usefulness of this skill for any dog, anywhere, your reactive dog will hugely benefit. See the Resources section for details.

Watchpoint

Teaching calm and relaxation is *not* teaching a stay exercise (although you will get a solid stay as a result) with the traditional stern shouting and finger-waving. The object is quite different - to change your dog's mental state, not to anchor his physical position.

Learning how to switch off can also help with Separation Anxiety. This is not the place to go through a program for changing this area of distress in your dog, but the Resources section holds some answers for you.

In passing, I'll also mention the Relaxation Protocol (Resources section again). This is a program which takes incremental steps from frantic non-resting dog to chilled-out dog with a lower heart-rate and dreamy feelings of comfort and relaxation. It's a simple program: you don't have to do Day 1 only on Day 1 - repeat each "Day" till you have it right, then move on to the next "Day". It takes time, yes, but it's time well spent helping your dog de-stress. You'll feel as if you've had a relaxation session yourself! It's worth getting started on it to help your dog access the calm side of his mind, which he may have lost sight of in his anxiety.

De-stressing

If you get a fright, your hormones come to your body's rescue and flood the system with what is needed to restore calm. Cortisol provides fuel for fight or flight and is essential to get us out of danger. But if the stressful or frightening stimulus continues or re-occurs, too much cortisol will be circulating, which can lead to longer-term ailments. Imagine if you had a minor car crash. Even though you weren't hurt, your cortisol levels will have shot up. You need a couple of days for them to settle again. Until then you could be very jumpy as soon as you get in a car, or even try to cross the road. It's an unpleasant feeling, and we naturally try to soothe any friend or relative who has had a fright. Rest and tea and nursery food are in order!

Your dog, yet again, is the same! If when walking, he kicks up a fuss at a passing dog, he has just gone through the same experience as you in your car crash. His hormone levels are raised - he's more likely to react to the next dog. Your walk is not now remotely pleasurable! It's exhausting for both of you.

Your dog needs to get home to a safe place and relax and live a boring, uneventful, life for two to three days to allow the levels to go back to normal.

There is no law that dictates that your dog must be walked every day!

He needs exercise, sure, but that can be achieved in a fairly small garden, with some energetic games with a ball or a flirt pole. He needs mental stimulation - yes. But that can be achieved by playing some games involving searching and nosework, tricks, or food-toys.

In general, walks are social outings - essential for young puppies - but they're not exercise. Free running and jumping about till your dog's sides are heaving, his tongue lolling, and his eyes shining, are what you want for exercise.

So, if no-one is enjoying these walks, don't do 'em! You'll be getting tools and techniques from me to transform your dog into a more detached and thoughtful creature. Then you'll be looking for walks with plenty of dogs around to practice your new skills!

Medication

I'll just mention this here briefly, as we looked at meds in more detail in Book 1. I am not (as you know by now) a vet. So you must do your own homework. But there is no shame in getting meds for your dog if that's what he needs in order to lead a normal life. You can start with the herbal-type over-the-counter remedies before upgrading to the class A stuff. These seem to work well with some dogs, and not at all with others, so just try them and see. They also tend to kick in much faster than the prescription drugs. Those that are marketed as fireworks remedies obviously have to start working quickly. You may like to consider visiting a Veterinary Behaviourist before taking this step.

In this chapter we have learnt:

- The importance of rest and sleep for your reactive dog
- The difference between exercise and social walking
- That you don't have to keep up dogwalks if your dog finds them unpleasant
- Meds may help him till his new skills become automatic

Chapter 10
Distance revisited

We took a look at the sophisticated language dogs use to converse in Book 1. We're going to take another look at it here from a different angle: how to use your knowledge of this to your advantage on walks. And it's appearing as another new Action Step, just in case Action Step 9 in Book 1 slipped past you ...

ACTION STEP 24:

This step is critical! *Show your dog she never has to meet another dog or person ever again.* When you and your dog see something coming that you know will upset her, you say a cheery "Let's go!", turn, and head in another direction. Your reward will be the relief you see in her face.

This is one of the most important moments for you to capture - the moment your dog sees another dog, causing a transformation in her whole body posture. She can go from relaxed and curvy to stiff and tense in the blink of an eye. Your eye, that is! If she's worried she may well be unable to give the calming signal of a soft blink or a lookaway. So you help her. Keeping your hands soft and your shoulders relaxed, you make a happy distracting noise and head off purposefully - elsewhere.

You've learnt that walking straight towards another dog is very poor form and can be misconstrued as aggressive. So why would you do this? Answer: because man has made lovely straight footpaths, roads, and pavements for us all to walk along! Left to their own devices, dogs will greet in a nonchalant, curvy, fashion. The size of the curve and the distance from each other depends on a number of factors, which may include relative size, age, sex, and manner.

So without climbing a tree or scrambling over a wall into someone's garden, our only choice to avoid advancing straight towards another dog is to turn and go. This is not a dramatic, screaming, exit! It's a gentle curve away - as softly as you can manage.

Note that many of our pavements and footpaths are more like tunnels! There may be hedges, walls, and fences down one side; there may be parked cars down the other. Being in a tunnel makes the fight or flight response kick in much faster. Imagine walking down a narrow alleyway one dark night and you see a suspicious character lurking halfway along. You are definitely going to feel trapped, and maybe start panicking. This is how your dog feels!

Remember that a dog's personal space requirement is way bigger than ours.

The fourth emergency measure!

This is your "get out of jail" card promised in Chapter 8 of this book. This will be invaluable to you to remove your dog instantly from a situation she may not even be aware of. Whereas in Action Step 24 above, you need your dog to be aware of the oncoming hazard so she can appreciate your speedy response in getting her out of trouble, in this Key Lead Skill you can act before she's even seen it. Invaluable for when a dog suddenly appears from nowhere just a few yards ahead!

Key Lead Skill no. 6
Emergency Turn "Happy"

1. You are walking with your dog on lead beside you
2. You see an imaginary hazard up ahead
3. Stop (your dog will feel this on the lead) as you call out "Happy!"
4. Your dog will turn to see what's going on
5. Back up, smiling and connecting with your dog as she comes towards you, and you run backwards
6. When you have her full attention, turn and head away briskly with her beside you
7. Finish the sequence with a treat as you walk away from the hazard

Play this game frequently. Your dog should get to love this and be very quick: "Ha, you can't catch me out!" Nine times out of ten play it as a game - only occasionally will you use it for real. Be sure to go back to playing it as a game once you've used it in earnest: you don't want your dog thinking that "Happy!" means "Danger! Dog incoming!" As a nice spin-off, you'll find her paying more attention to you as you walk - just in case you start this game!

Why that loopy word "Happy!"? It's very hard to say "Happy!" while looking worried or sounding angry. When your dog turns to look at you, isn't it better that she sees her lovely owner looking happy? You also have to consider the person with the dog coming towards you. If you yell the dog's name, they may react by trying to haul their dog away from this mad person with their dangerous dog and set up a chain of events you want to avoid! And if your dog's name is Chappie, or Mattie, or something that sounds too like Happy, try "Smiley!". Of course you can use any word or sound you want, but using a word that will influence the outcome is handy. I am indebted to one of my students - Janet, with her Leonberger Chloe - who came up with this ingenious and effective word.

ACTION STEP 25:

Learn the Emergency Turn inside out, till you can initiate it at a second's notice. If you practice it daily, not only will your dog get very quick at it, but you will have it honed and ready for when you need it, without first panicking, clutching the lead and wondering what to do!

In this chapter we've learnt that:

- Distance is our friend
- You always need to keep an eye on your distance
- If that distance shrinks too much, you can get away swiftly and painlessly
- We are Happy!

Chapter 11
Managing walks

Equipment

In Chapter 1 of this book we looked at equipment in detail. In addition to the right gear, you now have six Key Lead Skills to help you. As you are by now getting used to your dog's new kit, you will also - as a team - be getting very fluent at those lead skills.

Consider these skills a priority. Gentle handling is key to making your walks pleasant and uneventful. Think of the ace showjumper: his hands are soft, his use of the reins sympathetic. If he keeps sawing at his horse's mouth, the animal will get a "hard mouth" and become unresponsive to a light touch on the reins. In the same way, your dog can get a "hard neck" from all the lead-jabbing that has been going on, and you have to hoist him into the middle of next week for him to notice a touch on the lead.

Working together with your dog, your gentle pressure on the lead being echoed by his gentle pressure in return, will help to bring you the results you want.

> ACTION STEP 26:
>
> Re-visit Chapter 1 of this book and ensure you have ditched any aversive gear and replaced it with effective, friendly, safe, and helpful, equipment that you are both enjoying using.

A word about car reactivity

Sometimes, just getting to your walking place is fraught with hazards! Your dog barks at everything he sees on the car journey, be it dog, horse, person, child, bike … So by the time you arrive, your dog is already in a highly aroused state, twitchy and ready to bark at the next thing he sees.

So consider what you can do to make your car rides more peaceful - not to mention safer. A dog leaping about in the car barking is not helping your concentration on the road!

What will usually make a huge difference is restricting your dog's vision. If he can't see it, he can't bark at it. Obviously he needs to be restrained in one area of the car for his safety - not to mention everyone else's. A loose dog in a car is deemed an "unsecured load" and is certainly against the law in the UK, and I suspect elsewhere as well. In an emergency stop, 50 lbs of dog hitting the back of your seat at 40 miles an hour is not going to do either of you any good. Personally, I favour robust, non-rattling, crates - which must have an escape door to the inside of the car in case of accident. I'm not convinced about the efficacy of dog seatbelt restraints and I'd never leave a dog tied up in the car unsupervised anyway - that's an accident waiting to happen, as he jumps off the seat getting his leg caught in the handbrake lever …

So now there are three possibilities:

1. Cover the crate. With a dark cloth, cover the crate so that your dog can't see out of the window. Leave plenty of space for air circulation lower in the crate.

2. Cover the windows near your dog's place in the car. You could do all the back windows - you can't, of course cover the front windows! But a curtain dividing front from back may work for you. A quick and easy way to cover the windows is to use black-out material or strongly-patterned fabric. Choose one that doesn't fray and you won't even need to hem it. To fix the panels over the windows, you can use either velcro dots (put the fuzzy side on the car and the spiky side on the fabric), or hem in tiny magnets which will attach themselves readily to the metal of the car window frame. You can throw these up very quickly, then rip them down just as quickly when you are carrying hoomins*.

    *LOLspeak for people, in case you're not familiar with the term!

3. Another option that works well with some dogs is a Calming Cap - a kind of soft mask you fit over your dog's face which makes the world appear fuzzy and unresolved. Naturally you'd acclimatise your dog to this first, using the same method you'll see to teach a dog to love his muzzle (in the Resources section). Remember we want our dog to be less stressed, not more stressed, so for some dogs this may be a no-no.

Those Key Lead Skills

ACTION STEP 27:

Get the Key Lead Skills you found in Chapters 4 and 10 of this book fluent and easy. If you have poor motor skills or you just struggle with left and right, practice with a friend. Children will be happy to volunteer to "be a dog" for you! Once these skills are a firm habit, walks will be so much easier!

So use a long line where appropriate, keep your hands soft, and keep your distance! You'll need to be very familiar with all these skills before embarking on the techniques coming up.

Muzzle

We've frequently visited muzzles so far in this book - in Chapter 1, Chapter 3, Action Step 18, and Chapter 8.

The key points are that a muzzle

- keeps people away
- helps you relax

If you feel more relaxed knowing for certain your biting dog cannot bite anything, go for it!

ACTION STEP 28:

Shed your pre-conceptions. Do what is right for your dog.

Incoming dog!

This is the bane of many a dog-owner's existence! The loose, rampaging dog. Hearing the owner in the distance calling out "It's ok, he's friendly," is no help whatever. And perhaps the dog is ownerless, or virtually ownerless, as his owner slopes off, shoulders hunched, talking on the phone, no interest in his dog who, in any case, has zero recall. The owner knows this and isn't about to demonstrate his miserable training failure to you! So asking the person to call their dog is more often than not fruitless.

What can you do? Here are a number of things you can try. Nothing is guaranteed to work, but in my experience using one or more of these tactics you can usually escape unscathed. Remember the other dog is not to blame for his unruly behaviour: it's not his fault he has no training. So treat him with the same kindness you'd want for your own dog.

- First thing, as ever, is distance. Turn on your heel, using Key Lead Skills 5 and/or 6, and march smartly away, chatting to your dog

- And the other first thing is to relax your hands on the lead! Nothing transmits fear as quickly as the lead being yanked and your dog half-strangled

- Collar hold (see Chapter 1 of this book). I call my reactive dog over to me as I see an incoming dog and slip my hand in her loose collar, the back of my hand lying against her neck. She relaxes and waits beside me. If we're so calm that we're utterly boring, the other dog often gives up and heads off. (But if required Lacy can give a magnificent withering stare which will intimidate many dogs!)

- "The House is on Fire!": Emergency Recall x 10. Yell excitedly at your dog while you turn and race away fast. The surprise element can often work

- If you have a companion, teach them to call out "Incoming!" as soon as they see something heading your way, giving you time to decide on your exit strategy

- If your dog is genuinely ok off-lead (are you absolutely sure?) and incomer doesn't look dangerous, drop the lead while you keep away. Don't interfere. This may surprise you!

- Some people have success tossing a handful of treats at the dog as he arrives. I wouldn't do that if the dog looked ferocious and may misinterpret my arm action!

- If you have a walking stick or staff, swing it *gently* back and forth like a pendulum in front of you and your dog. This is *odd* and may cause the incomer to back off. You're not trying to hit the dog!

- No staff? Try twirling your lead round in a big circle, like a windmill. Ensure any metal bits are in your hand. You don't, of course, want to hurt the dog, and you certainly don't want to whack your ankle with a lead clasp. Again, a slow circle is odd enough to get most nosy dogs away. Practice this first

- A pop-up umbrella - the type where you press a button and it opens - can be very handy, especially if you have a small dog. Ping it open in front of your dog. This will at the very least give pause to the rushing incomer. If it's a sighthound racing in intent on your small fluffy this may well be a lifesaver

- With the swinging staff, the windmill lead, and the umbrella, teach your own dog at home first, and associate this new game of yours with treats and good things

- Small dog: you may be tempted to pick him up. This could work, but equally it could cause the incomer (who was only nosy) to grab this fluffy toy as you swing it up in the air. Then your arm may get bitten too. You grabbing your dog can also make your dog more afraid - and as you bend, your face will be at incoming dog tooth level: not good. So teach your little dog to jump into your arms instead.

- Gadgets like air horns and aversive sprays: *wah-wah*. This is blanket bombing that will affect your dog as well as the incomer, making him more frightened than ever. Skip them.

- Ignore the abuse you will quite possibly get from the other owner. I have been accused of kicking or hitting their dog (never), of enticing their dog away on purpose (?!), and of being unable to control my (leashed) dog while their (loose) dog snapped at his face. They know they're in the wrong, and they try to cover their confusion and embarrassment by going on the offensive. And it can sure be offensive sometimes as the air turns blue! The abusers have always been male. Just sayin'.

ACTION STEP 29:

Practice any of these suggestions you like the look of when there is no threat. Make it a fun game for your dog, so she's a willing partner.

Loose Lead Walking

How on earth can teaching my dog to walk nicely on the lead beside me help with managing her reactivity on walks? Easy!

- It gives her a position she is secure in, and where she can look up and see your face
- It's a party trick she can depend upon to produce rewards
- It gives her a focus - something to be doing other than scanning the horizon for approaching hazards
- It puts you into a companionable bubble with your dog as you walk through the world together

> ### ACTION STEP 30:
>
> For a complete program on achieving this, go to the third book in the series **Essential Skills for a Brilliant Family Dog**: *Let's Go! Enjoy Companionable Walks with your Brilliant Family Dog* (for where to find this step-by-step book, check the Resources section).

Wide open spaces

Choose your area carefully! There are cultural differences about off-lead walking, so you need to know what the position is in your neck of the woods. Here in the UK we enjoy freedom with our dogs on the vast network of public footpaths and bridle paths hallowed by history, nationally-owned forests, many beaches, Areas of Outstanding Natural Beauty, national parks, and - of course, farmers' fields with permission.

This may not be an option in some countries - but there has to be somewhere you can take your dog and enjoy free running. As this is an essential freedom for your pet - enshrined in law in the UK and I'm sure many other enlightened countries - perhaps it's time for you to do a bit of civil agitating and ensure proper facilities for dogs to enjoy full physical and mental health.

Having the right to this freedom does not absolve you of responsibility for your dog! But having a wide open space where you can see a long way will make minding your dog miles easier. You have early warning of anything untoward, and your dog can enjoy watching other people and dogs at a distance, maybe hundreds of yards, without fear.

If your dog is a maniac for his toy - so much the better. Always provided he's not guardy over it, of course. If you can't presently guarantee distraction by offering to toss a ball or frisbee, this is a skill you want to develop!

As always on walks, avoid tunnels - narrow alleyways of buildings or hedgerows, narrow streets with tunnels of garden walls and parked cars, narrow footpaths.

Where are we going with this?

So far I have given you lots of background to what your dog is about (Book 1) and lots of tricks and techniques for you to learn (Book 2). It may have surprised you that I go into such detail with things that may not at first appear to be directly linked to your problems. But you don't start your child on trigonometry and calculus! You start with moving counters around and exploring concepts of bigger and smaller. So you need to look at why your dog does what he does first. There's nothing I've given you in these two books that I feel could be omitted. It's a holistic approach to understanding and treating reactivity.

In Book 3 we'll be getting down to the nitty-gritty and exploring methods that have been proven to work to lower stress, anxiety, fear, and frustration, in your dog. These methods will, of course, all be force-free. There is no place for force, intimidation, or coercion in a loving relationship.

Just as a trailer - a cliffhanger for you! - these are broadly the areas you can look forward to covering:

Counter-conditioning and De-sensitisation

Control Unleashed (Leslie McDevitt) - specifically "Look at That"

BAT (Behavior Adjustment Training - Grisha Stewart) in all its glory

By all means purchase the relevant books (see Resources section) if you want to go into great detail with them. They are excellent. But if you're like me, you don't want to buy a car manual and get under the bonnet with a spanner!

You'd rather a mechanic translated it for you into what you need to know and can relate to. I'm going to make it all very accessible and give you what you need to have success, step by step, just as I give it to my students in person.

"Thanks very much for your time and help. I was really glad to see how well Dexter responded today. It has given me the confidence to help him. Dex and I will enjoy our exercises and getting to know one another."
Debbie and Dexter, Border Collie, anxious, over-wrought

"Sam's doing really well - he's much happier all round which is fab."
Ashleigh and Sam, Border Collie rescue, super fearful of everything, at home and out

"Both dogs are doing really well, Coco is so much better going out for a walk and Rocky has calmed down. Thank you so much for all your help."
Sharon with Coco and Rocky, Jack Russell Terriers, highly reactive and noisy!

In this chapter we have learnt:

- More about walk management, including escapes and incoming dogs
- How to minimise car reactivity
- The importance of the Action Steps from the earlier chapters
- There is exciting stuff coming!

Conclusion

We've travelled a long way on our journey into the whys and wherefores and the what-can-you-do-about-its of your reactive and anxious dog. We've covered:

- What equipment you should have or shun
- The anatomy of rewards and rewarding
- Building confidence - for you and your dog
- Critical lead skills
- Choice training plus a bit of science if you want it
- How to manage walks, distance, and escape
- Relaxation

You are well on the way to enjoying a far calmer relationship with your dog. The future does not look so grim. Now you not only understand more about why what's happening is happening, but you have techniques and strategies to change things!

You should be noticing big changes already.

Maybe you're wondering when we're going to get down to brass tacks and learn more techniques to help you - wonder no longer! In the next book we'll be going into detail to help you achieve your goals of having a calm and "normal" dog (what's normal anyway?), a dog you can rely on, a dog you can easily manage, and a dog you can enjoy.

Appreciation

I want to offer thanks to all those who have helped me get where I am in my life with dogs:

- First of all, my own long-suffering dogs! They have taught me so much when I've taken the time to listen.
- My reactive dog Lacy who is a star and has opened up a new world for me.
- My students, who have shown me how they learn best, enabling me to give them what they need to know in a way that works for them.
- Some legendary teachers, principal amongst them: Sue Ailsby, Leslie McDevitt, Grisha Stewart, Chirag Patel, Susan Garrett. I wholeheartedly recommend them. They are trailblazers.

Resources

You know now that there's light at the end of this tunnel! And to discover that the tunnel is much shorter than you think, get the next two parts of the puzzle here:

Essential Skills for your *Growly* but Brilliant Family Dog series
Book 1 **Why is my Dog so Growly?** *Teach your fearful, aggressive, or reactive dog confidence through understanding*
Book 3 **Calm walks with your Growly Dog** *Strategies and techniques for your fearful, aggressive, or reactive dog*

For a very thorough, in-depth, approach, where I will be on hand to answer all your questions, go to

brilliantfamilydog.teachable.com

where you'll find info about the online course which takes all this to the next level, giving you personal support and encouragement as well as all the lessons and techniques you need to change your life with your Growly Dog.

For a free taster course: **www.brilliantfamilydog.com/growly**

And for loads of articles on Growly Dogs and Choice Training, go to **www.brilliantfamilydog.com** where you'll also find a course on solving everyday dog and puppy problems.

You'll also find the **Essential Skills for a Brilliant Family Dog** series of e-books helpful. Take a holistic view of your relationship with your dog and work on new skills inside the house as well as when you're out. If your dog has always had to be kept on lead because you were afraid he was not safe, you'll definitely need Book 4 for your new life!

Book 1 Calm Down! *Step-by-Step to a Calm, Relaxed, and Brilliant Family Dog*
Book 2 Leave it! *How to teach Amazing Impulse Control to your Brilliant Family Dog*
Book 3 Let's Go! *Enjoy Companionable Walks with your Brilliant Family Dog*
Book 4 Here Boy! *Step-by-step to a Stunning Recall from your Brilliant Family Dog*

And you'll be pleased to know that Book 1 is currently free at all e-book stores!

Here are the links to all the resources mentioned in this book:

Books by other authors:

I'll Be Home Soon: How to Prevent and Treat Separation Anxiety by Patricia McConnell, pub First Stone, 2010

Control Unleashed: Creating a Focused and Confident Dog by Leslie McDevitt, pub Clean Run Productions LLC, 2007 http://controlunleashed.net/book.html

Behavior Adjustment Training 2.0: New Practical Techniques for Fear, Frustration, and Aggression in Dogs by Grisha Stewart, pub Dogwise Publishing, 2016

Dog Tricks: Fun and Games for Your Clever Canine by Mary Ray and Justine Harding, pub Hamlyn 2005

Brain Games for Dogs: Fun ways to build a strong bond with your dog and provide it with vital mental stimulation by Claire Arrowsmith, pub Firefly Books, 2010

101 Dog Tricks: Step by Step Activities to Engage, Challenge, and Bond with Your Dog by Kyra Sundance, Quarry Books, 2007

Websites:

www.muzzleupproject.com - all things muzzle

www.goodfordogs.co.uk/products - Wiggles Wags and Whiskers Freedom Harness - UK and Europe [This is me. If you buy from me I will benefit financially, but it won't cost you any more.]

http://2houndswholesale.com/Where-to-Buy.html - Wiggles Wags and Whiskers Freedom Harness - rest of the world

https://www.youtube.com/watch?v=1OHEB41yRdU - one of many calming sound recordings

https://positively.com/dog-wellness/dog-enrichment/music-for-dogs/canine-noise-phobia-series/ - for desensitisation

http://en.turid-rugaas.no/calming-signals---the-art-of-survival.html - dog body language

http://championofmyheart.com/relaxation-protocol-mp3-files/ audio files for the Relaxation Protocol

http://www.thundershirt.com - for Thundershirt and Calming Cap

https://www.youtube.com/watch?v=Mtn-BeI9lHE - *Pattern Games: Clicking for Confidence and Connection* by Leslie McDevitt, dvd 2011, Tawzer Dog LLC

https://www.youtube.com/watch?v=UGcyier95sw - watch dogs drive cars and fly planes! Really!

http://www.thekennelclub.org.uk/kcdog - KC Dog: section of the UK Kennel Club devoted to protecting dogs' rights

Force-free training hubs:

http://www.apdt.co.uk/dog-owners/local-dog-trainers - UK resource for force-free trainers http://www.petprofessionalguild.com/PetGuildMembers - global resource for force-free trainers

http://grishastewart.com/cbati-directory/ - global resource for specialist Certified BAT Instructors

Alternative practitioner societies:

www.ttouch.com

www.ttouchtteam.co.uk

www.k9-massageguild.co.uk

www.massageawareness.com

www.caninebowentechnique.com

Works consulted for Chapter 6:

http://www.britannica.com/biography/Sigmund-Freud accessed 2016

Mischel, W., et al. (1989). *Delay of gratification in children.* Science, 24 4 (4907), 933–938

https://www.apa.org/helpcenter/willpower-gratification.pdf accessed 2016

Casey, B. J., et al. (2011). *Behavioral and neural correlates of delay of gratification 40 years later.* Proceedings of the National Academy of Sciences, 10 8 (36), 14998–15003

http://www.nobelprize.org/nobel_prizes/medicine/laureates/1904/pavlov-bio.html accessed 2016

http://psychology.about.com/od/classicalconditioning/a/pavlovs-dogs.htm accessed 2016

Skinner, B.F. (1938) *The Behavior of Organisms: An Experimental Analysis,* New York; Appleton-Century

Skinner, B.F. (1951) *"How to teach animals"* Scientific American

Reynolds, G.S. (1968), *A Primer of Operant Conditioning.* Palo Alto, California: Scott, Foresman

Bailey, B, and M.B. Bailey (1996) *Patient Like the Chipmunks.* Eclectic Science Productions

http://www.clickertraining.com/karen accessed 2016

Mary R. Burch and Jon S. Bailey (1999), *How Dogs Learn*, Wiley, NY

Don't go without your free book!

Impulse Control is particularly valuable for the reactive and anxious dog. Get a head start with your training by developing astonishing self-control in your dog! Change your dog from quick on the trigger, to thoughtful and reflective.

Go now and get your step-by-step book absolutely free at
Brilliant Family Dog
www.brilliantfamilydog.com/freebook-growly

About the author

I've been training dogs for many years. First for competitive dog sports and over time to be stellar family pets. For most of my life, I've lived with up to four dogs, so I'm well used to getting a multi-dog household to run smoothly. It soon became clear that a force-free approach was by far the most successful, effective, and rewarding for me and the dogs. I've done the necessary studying for my various qualifications - for rehab of anxious and fearful "aggressive" dogs, early puppy development, and learning theory and its practical applications. I am continually studying and learning this endlessly amazing subject!

There are some superb teachers and advocates of force-free dog training, and you'll find those I am particularly indebted to in the Appreciation Section. Some of the methods I show you are well-known in the force-free dog training community, while many have my own particular twist.

A lot of my learning has come through the Puppy Classes, Puppy Walks, and Growly Dog Courses I teach. These dog-owners are not looking for competition-standard training; they just want a Brilliant Family Dog they can take anywhere. It's a particular joy for me to see a Growly Dog who arrived at the first session a reactive bundle of nerves and fear, who ends up able to cope with almost anything the world chucks his way - becoming a relaxed and happy dog with a confident owner in the process.

Working with real dogs and their real owners keeps me humble - and resourceful! It's no good being brilliant at training dogs if you can't convey this enthusiasm and knowledge to the person the dog has to live with. So I'm grateful for everything my students have taught me about how they learn best.

Beverley Courtney BA(Hons) CBATI CAP2 MAPDT(UK) PPG
www.brilliantfamilydog.com

Made in United States
North Haven, CT
19 October 2022

25652629R00082